PHILOSOPHY OF MIND

GW00497626

BASICS

Philosophy of Mind: The Basics is a concise and engaging introduction to the fundamental philosophical questions and theories about the mind. The author Amy Kind, a leading expert in the field, examines central issues concerning the nature of consciousness, thought, and emotion. The book addresses key questions such as:

- What is the nature of the mind?
- What is the relationship between the mind and the brain?
- Can machines have minds?
- How will future technology impact the mind?

With a glossary of key terms and suggestions for further reading, *Philosophy of Mind: The Basics* is an ideal starting point for anyone seeking a lively and accessible introduction to the rich and complex study of philosophy of mind.

Amy Kind is Russell K. Pitzer Professor of Philosophy at Claremont McKenna College, USA. She is editor of *Philosophy of Mind in the Twentieth and Twenty-First Centuries* (volume six of *The History of the Philosophy of Mind*, Routledge 2016) and of *The Routledge Handbook of Philosophy of Imagination* (2016). She has also authored the introductory textbook *Persons and Personal Identity* (2015).

ENFIELD LIBRARIES 09/21

9120000748784

The Basics

American Philosophy
Nancy Stanlick

Animal Ethics
Tony Milligan

Artificial Intelligence
Kevin Warwick

Evolution
Sherrie Lyons

Food Ethics
Ronald Sandler

Free will
Meghan Griffith

Metaphysics
Michael Rae

Philosophy (fifth edition)
Nigel Warburton

Global Justice
Carl Death and Huw L. Williams

Human Genetics (second edition)
Ricki Lewis

Logic (second edition)
J.C. Beall

Bioethics (second edition)
Alastair Campbell

Eastern Philosophy (second edition)
Victoria Harrison

Phenomenology
Dan Zahavi

Atheism
Graham Oppy

Emotion
Michael Brady

Other titles in the series can be found at: https://www.routledge.com/The-Basics/book-series/B

PHILOSOPHY OF MIND

THE BASICS

Amy Kind

Routledge
Taylor & Francis Group
LONDON AND NEW YORK

First published 2020
by Routledge
2 Park Square, Milton Park, Abingdon, Oxon OX14 4RN

and by Routledge
52 Vanderbilt Avenue, New York, NY 10017

Routledge is an imprint of the Taylor & Francis Group, an informa business

British Library Cataloguing in Publication Data
A catalogue record for this book is available from the British Library

Library of Congress Cataloging-in-Publication Data
Names: Kind, Amy, author.
Title: Philosophy of mind : the basics / Amy Kind. Description: Abingdon Oxon ; New York, NY : Routledge, 2020. | Includes bibliographical references and index.
Identifiers: LCCN 2019051831 (print) | LCCN 2019051832 (ebook) | ISBN 9781138807815 (hardback) | ISBN 9781138807822 (paperback) | ISBN 9781315750903 (ebook)
Subjects: LCSH: Philosophy of mind.
Classification: LCC BD418.3 .K564 2020 (print) | LCC BD418.3 (ebook) | DDC 128/.2–dc23 LC record available at https://lccn.loc.gov/2019051831
LC ebook record available at https://lccn.loc.gov/2019051832

ISBN: 978-1-138-80781-5 (hbk)
ISBN: 978-1-138-80782-2 (pbk)
ISBN: 978-1-315-75090-3 (ebk)

Typeset in Bembo
by Taylor & Francis Books

CONTENTS

ACKNOWLEDGEMENTS

My first real interaction with philosophy of mind came as an undergraduate at Amherst College. I took my first philosophy of mind course from Jyl Gentzler, and I wrote my undergraduate thesis on the Chinese Room thought experiment under the supervision of Alex George. Their teaching continues to influence me to this day. As a graduate student at UCLA, I benefited from classes and conversations on issues in philosophy of mind with Joseph Almog and Tyler Burge, as well as fellow graduate students such as Torin Alter and Mike Jacovides. Serving as a TA for Dana Nelkin's summer course on philosophy of mind proved hugely influential for how I would myself go on to teach that class.

Over my years of teaching at Claremont McKenna College, my thinking about the issues discussed in this book has been further shaped by my interactions with the many wonderful undergraduates who have taken my introductory courses and my courses on Philosophy of Mind and Philosophy Through Science Fiction. They also help me to keep updating my television and movie references, though I'm probably never going to stop making reference to *Star Trek*. Recently, Dri Tattersfield '21 read a draft of several chapters of the book and offered useful feedback that helped me to make the book more user-friendly.

At various times over the years, friends and colleagues have given me feedback on some of the chapters of this book and/or discussed some of the issues with me. I won't try to name them all now for fear of forgetting someone. The philosophy hive mind on social media gave me several good suggestions for further reading. Robert Howell gave me particularly good advice on some key issues as I was finalizing the manuscript, and Brandon Polite sent me extremely helpful comments on the entire draft manuscript. I am also very grateful to the five anonymous referees who reviewed my original proposal for this book and to the three anonymous referees who reviewed the draft manuscript. The book is much better as a result of their comments.

As always, my deepest thanks go to my husband Frank Menetrez, and my two sons, Stephen and Joseph.

MIND AND MENTALITY

In *Harry Potter and the Order of the Phoenix*, the fifth book in J.K. Rowling's Harry Potter series, Harry finally kisses Cho, a classmate on whom he has had a crush since his early days at Hogwarts School of Witchcraft and Wizardry. Unfortunately, however, Cho starts crying during the kiss. Were Cho's tears a sign that Harry is a terrible kisser? That's the explanation that Harry and Ron come up with when discussing the situation afterwards. In an effort to set them straight, Hermione tries to get them to understand how things likely seem from Cho's perspective:

> Well, obviously, she's feeling very sad, because of Cedric dying. Then I expect she's feeling confused because she liked Cedric and now she likes Harry, and she can't work out who she likes best. Then she'll be feeling guilty, thinking it's an insult to Cedric's memory to be kissing Harry at all, and she'll be worrying about what everyone else might say about her if she starts going out with Harry. And she probably can't work out what her feelings toward Harry are anyway, because he was the one who was with Cedric when Cedric died, so that's all very mixed up and painful. Oh, and she's afraid she's going to be thrown off the Ravenclaw Quidditch team because she's been flying so badly.
>
> (Rowling 2014, 424)

When encountering Hermione's explanation, some readers might disagree with the accuracy of her assessment of Cho's feelings, while others might think she got things exactly right. Still others might share Ron's stunned reaction: "One person can't feel all that at once, they'd explode." Whichever of these reactions one has, however, the kinds of characterizations that Hermione uses to describe Cho – that she's thinking and feeling and worrying, that she has conflicting romantic inclinations, that she's sad and afraid and confused – are no doubt familiar ones. All of these characterizations seem a perfectly natural way to describe a teenager like Cho's states of mind.

Of course, Cho and the other students at Hogwarts are witches and wizards, but we use the same kinds of words to describe the states of mind of those of us humans who are not endowed with magical powers. But now suppose we take a step back and consider what exactly these descriptions are describing. What is a state of mind? Or, to step back even farther, what is a mind? Posing these questions provides an entry point into philosophy of mind, the subject matter that we'll be exploring in this book.

WHAT IS PHILOSOPHY OF MIND?

Philosophy of mind sits at the intersection of two big sub-fields of philosophy – **metaphysics** and **epistemology**. In metaphysics we take up questions about reality, and more specifically, about its structure and nature. We normally accept the existence of things like tables and trees and tadpoles without question. But do all of these things really exist, or are they just elaborate fictions imposed by human beings on the world? And what about other kinds of seeming existents, like time and numbers and God? Do all these exist too? And if so, how is their existence to be understood and explained, given that they aren't the kinds of things that we can see and touch?

While metaphysics concerns the structure and nature of reality, epistemology concerns the structure and nature of our *access* to reality. In particular, epistemology takes up questions about knowledge, belief, and justification. We normally take ourselves to have all sorts of beliefs about the world – that there's a table in the kitchen, that trees require sunlight to flourish, that tadpoles are baby frogs. In many cases, these are not just claims that we take ourselves to believe but claims that we take ourselves to know. But what differentiates knowledge from mere belief? In addition to knowing the existence of things that we see and touch like tables and trees and tadpoles, can we also know of the existence of things that we can't see and touch, like time and numbers and God? How do we gain such knowledge? And, given that our perceptual capacities are fallible and that we are often victims of illusions and hallucinations, is it even really possible for us to know of the existence of tables and trees and tadpoles?

Philosophy of mind addresses issues in both metaphysics and epistemology. On the metaphysics side, philosophers of mind ask: What is the nature of the mind? What is its relation to the brain and to the body? Which sorts of beings have minds? On the epistemological side, philosophers of mind ask: What methods of study can provide us with knowledge about the mind? Or, more specifically: Are introspective methods – methods where we draw upon our own inwardly-focused mental assessments – reliable? How can we know whether (and, if so, which) other beings have minds? Although we will explore both metaphysical and epistemological lines of inquiry in philosophy of mind throughout this book, our attention will primarily be focused on metaphysical matters.

The first two metaphysical questions just mentioned – *What is the nature of the mind?* and *What is its relation to the brain and body?* – are frequently referred to jointly as *the mind-body problem*. This problem came to prominence through the work of René Descartes, a 17th century French philosopher who is often thought of as the father of philosophy of mind. Much of the work in philosophy of mind in the centuries since has been devoted to the mind-body problem. This topic will occupy our attention in Chapters Two, Three, and Four of this book. Subsequent chapters will address these metaphysical questions through the lens of machine mentality and the place of mind in our increasingly technological world.

Before we can dive into those topics, however, it will be useful to lay some groundwork for the discussion. In the remainder of this chapter, we tackle three different subjects that will help to prepare us for the discussion to follow in the remainder of the book. The first main section offers an investigation of our mental life and, in particular, provides a survey of the different types of mental states for which a theory of mind will have to account. The second main section offers an exploration of the kinds of methodologies philosophers employ to study our mental life. The third section provides a schematic overview of philosophical theories of mind. Though several of these theories are explored in detail in subsequent chapters, it can be helpful to have a sense of the alternatives as one considers the advantages and disadvantages of each view. Arguments against one theory are often taken to be arguments for another, and so having a sense of the big picture puts one in a better position to evaluate each theory individually. Finally, in the last main section of this chapter, I provide a quick overview of the contents of the remainder of the book.

AN INVENTORY OF OUR MENTAL LIFE

At any given moment, even one in which you're sitting completely still, there are many things going on in your body. Your heart and circulatory system are pumping blood, your respiratory system is regulating your breathing, your digestive system is processing the contents of your most recent meal, and so on. At any given moment, there are also many things going on in your mind. Even if you're not experiencing quite the jumble of thoughts that Cho was when Harry kissed her, you're probably thinking and feeling many things all at the same time. Just consider a typical moment in the life of a student in a college class. As he stares at his professor's Power-Point slides and listens intently to what she's saying, determined to process every word, he might also be worrying about the exam he has tomorrow, remembering the fun time he had with friends last night, fighting off an intense wave of exhaustion, and trying to ignore a persistent itch on his left arm.

PROPOSITIONAL ATTITUDES

Consider the claim: *it's sunny today in Southern California*. We can take many different kinds of mental stances towards this claim. I might *believe* that it's sunny today in Southern California, *hope* that it's sunny today in Southern California, *dread* that it's sunny today in Southern California, and so on. Beliefs, desires, hopes, and dreads are mental states that philosophers refer to as **propositional attitudes**, so called because they consist in our taking a particular kind of attitude toward a certain kind of content, i.e., a proposition.

Now consider various different beliefs that someone might have: the belief that Arsenal is currently playing a match against Sheffield United, the belief that Arsenal is losing, and the belief that people in the United States refer to the game that they're playing as "soccer" while people in the United Kingdom refer to the game that they're playing as "football." Each of these beliefs is representational, as each of them represents or is about events or states of affairs in the world. In fact, all propositional attitudes are representational mental states. Whether I believe or desire or hope or dread that Arsenal win today's game, my mental states can be said to be *about* or *directed at* a certain event currently happening in the world. Philosophers refer to this phenomenon of representationality or aboutness as **intentionality**. "Intentionality" is here a technical word, and in this technical sense, it doesn't have anything to do with purposefulness. Whether a mental state has intentionality in the sense we're now talking about is completely independent of whether the mental state was deliberately or voluntarily formed.

Sometimes we have propositional attitudes that, though they can be described as being directed, cannot really be described as being directed *at the world*. Rather, they are directed at non-existent entities or states of affairs. Even in these sorts of cases, however, the mental state is about something and so has intentionality. Consider a child who desires to be as strong as Wonder Woman, or who worries that he will be attacked by the Loch Ness Monster, or who believes that Wonder Woman would emerge victorious were she to battle the Loch Ness Monster. Even though Wonder Woman and the Loch Ness Monster don't really exist, the child's desire, worry, and belief have intentionality nonetheless.

Some philosophers have claimed that all mental states are intentional. Indeed, some philosophers have even suggested that having intentionality is a distinguishing mark of the mental – it's what makes a state a mental state. Compare your mental state of believing that chocolate ice cream is delicious to the state that your stomach is in as it digests the chocolate ice cream or the state that your chin is in when it is covered by chocolate ice cream. All of these states involve chocolate ice cream, but only the mental state represents the chocolate ice cream. The view that intentionality is the mark of the mental is perhaps most closely associated with 19th century German philosopher Franz Brentano (1874), and the claim that all mental states are intentional has recently been defended by a number of philosophers of mind known as *intentionalists* or *representationalists*. But this claim is a controversial one, and as we will see, there are various mental states that seem to serve as counterexamples to this intentionalist claim.

Though beliefs and desires are both propositional attitudes, they are importantly different kinds of mental states. Compare your belief that there is chocolate ice cream in the freezer with your desire that there is chocolate ice cream in the freezer. Although both of these propositional attitudes represent the state of affairs that there is chocolate ice cream in the freezer, they do so in different ways. But how do we capture this difference? Here the philosophical notion of **direction of fit** is often introduced.

Beliefs have what's called a *mind-to-world* direction of fit. When we believe something, we aim to represent the world as it is (or as we take it to be), and we thus aim to conform the content of our mental state to the world. If, for example, you were to discover that your roommate ate all the chocolate ice cream that had previously been in the freezer, you would give up your belief that there's chocolate ice cream in the freezer. In contrast, when we desire something, we do not aim to represent the world as it is. Rather, we aim to adjust the world so that it conforms to the content of the mental state. A discovery that there is no chocolate ice cream in the freezer does not prompt you to give up the desire. Instead, it's likely to prompt you to go to the store to buy some chocolate ice cream – or to send your roommate to do so! Desires thus have what's called a *world-to-mind* direction of fit. Of course, we are not always successful in these endeavors – sometimes our beliefs are untrue, and sometimes our desires go unsatisfied. But these aims are central to making the relevant mental state the kind of mental state that it is.

Each of us has lots of beliefs and desires – lots and lots of beliefs and desires. Consider the desires you have about your own life. You want to be well fed, well educated, well liked, and so on... The list here will likely get pretty long pretty quickly and we haven't yet even begun to take into account the desires you have about other people's lives or the state of the world in general. Or consider the beliefs you have about world geography. You believe that Melbourne is south of Sydney, that Spain borders Portugal, that New York lies above the equator, and so on... Here again the list will likely get pretty long pretty quickly, and there are many, many other subject matters about which you likely have lots of beliefs.

At any given moment, however, very few of this vast number of beliefs and desires are present before your mind. Prior to reading the last paragraph, you were likely not actively thinking about the geographical relationship between Melbourne and Sydney or between Spain and Portugal. Or right now, before you go on to read the rest of this sentence, you are likely not actively thinking that Abraham Lincoln was the sixteenth President of the United States or that a triangle is a three-sided figure, even though these may very well be beliefs of yours. Philosophers thus distinguish between **occurrent** beliefs and desires and **non-occurrent** beliefs and desires. When you're taking a geography test about Australia, or trying to plan an Australian vacation, you might call up your belief about the geographical relationship between Sydney and Melbourne, and it becomes occurrent. Most of the time, however, this belief is non-occurrent.

FEELINGS: MOODS, EMOTIONS, SENSATIONS

In addition to propositional attitudes like beliefs and desires, we have many other kinds of mental states. One obvious class consists of moods and emotions, often referred to as *affective states*. You might be disgusted or surprised, angry or anxious, elated or depressed. How exactly to distinguish moods from emotions – indeed, even whether we should distinguish moods and emotions – is a vexed topic about which philosophers have had much to say. We will return to this topic in greater depth in Chapter Five, but for now, we'll settle for a rough characterization of the apparent difference: when the affective states are persistent and all pervasive, coloring everything one does, we tend to classify them as moods; when they are more short-lived or less all-encompassing, we tend to classify them as emotions. Recalling a piece of terminology that we saw earlier, emotions seem clearly to have intentionality, i.e., they are directed at or about a specific thing or event or state of affairs in the world. Someone might be happy that she got a promotion at work or, conversely, angry that she was passed over for a less-qualified candidate. But someone might be in an elated or depressed mood that's not about any particular thing or event – or even some collection of things or events. Rather, the mood seems best characterized as about nothing at all. In this way, moods seem non-intentional, or at least not as obviously intentional as emotions.

Indeed, moods serve as one of the standard counterexamples to the thesis we encountered earlier that all mental states have intentionality.

When talking about our emotions and moods, we often characterize them as feelings. It's not just that you are disgusted or surprised or angry or anxious but that you *feel* disgusted or surprised or angry or anxious. But emotions and moods do not exhaust the mental states that are characterized as feelings. In addition to feeling disgusted or surprised, you might also feel hungry or tired, or you might feel hot or in pain. Hunger, pain, and the like are not emotions or moods but rather *sensations*, or more specifically, *bodily sensations*.

At this point, however, one might feel somewhat uneasy. If feelings like hunger and pain are *bodily* sensations, then why should we count them as *mental* states? Perhaps the easiest way to address this question is to consider the phenomenon known as *phantom pain*. When someone experiences phantom pain, they feel painful sensations that seem to them to be localized in a specific body part, but the relevant body part no longer exists, usually due to amputation. Someone whose right arm has been amputated at the right elbow, for example, might have the sense that their right hand is uncomfortably clenched. In this case at least, we can't identify the pain as something happening in the right hand, since there is no right hand. More generally, then, we might think of pain as the mental experience of something that seems to be happening in one's body – and likewise for other bodily sensations.

There are yet other mental states that get characterized as feelings that don't seem to fall into either of these categories. Hermione describes Cho as feeling confused and mixed-up. Being mixed-up doesn't seem to be an emotion, but it also doesn't seem to be a sensation. So in addition to emotions and sensation, we want to leave room for a collection of states that we might simply think of as "other feelings" when we're taking inventory of our mental life.

PERCEPTUAL EXPERIENCE

We've so far canvassed several large classes of mental states: propositional attitudes, emotions and moods, bodily sensations, and other feelings. To this list we need also to add perceptions. As we engage the world we experience sights and sounds and smells and so on – all of which play a large role in our mental life. Moreover, though we're traditionally used to thinking of perception in terms of the five senses – sight, smell, taste, touch, and hearing – there is good evidence that human beings have additional senses as well. One prime candidate is proprioception – the sense we have of the relative positions of our own bodily parts. Even when you're just waking up in the morning and you haven't yet opened your eyes, you will still typically have a sense of where your arms are, for example. These proprioceptive states, just like visual states, count as a type of perception, broadly understood.

Perception is like belief in being intentional – our perceptual states are about things or states of affairs in the world. Perception is also like belief in having a mind-to-world direction of fit. When we perceive a state of affairs, we aim to conform our mind to the world as it is. Of course, however, we are not always successful in satisfying this aim. Not every time that we seem to see or hear something are we perceiving the world accurately. In some cases, though it seems to me that I see a cat hiding in the bushes, there is no cat hiding in the bushes. Rather, I'm suffering from an illusion or a hallucination. Or I might also be dreaming. These other perception-like states – which, like perception, are also intentional – need to be added to our mental state inventory as well. We will group them together with perceptions under the heading of *perceptual experiences*.

In addition to having intentionality, all of these perceptual experiences – whether they are perceptions or are merely perception-like – seem to have an additional important characteristic, namely, they are *qualitative* in nature. This point is also often put by saying that perceptual states have a *phenomenal feel* or that they are *phenomenally conscious* or that *there is something it is like* to have such states. The properties of mental states responsible for the phenomenal feel are often referred to as **qualia.** This is a plural term; to refer to one such property, philosophers use the singular form *quale*.

Consider the experience of seeing a strawberry lollipop. This experience has a different quality from the experience of seeing a lemon lollipop, and both of these experiences have a different quality from the experience of seeing a grape lollipop. Likewise for the experience of tasting a strawberry lollipop. This gustatory experience has a different qualitative nature from the experience of tasting a lemon lollipop or a grape lollipop. The experiences *feel* different from one another; *what's it's like* to have the one experience is different from *what it's like* to have the others.

With respect to their qualitative nature, perceptual states are quite unlike beliefs. It doesn't feel like anything to believe that two plus two equals four or that Abraham Lincoln was the 16th President of the United States. Here's another way to see the point. When you shift your gaze from viewing a strawberry lollipop to viewing a lemon lollipop, the character of your experience changes; it has a different feel. Yet when you've changed your mind about which flavor lollipop is your favorite, going from believing that strawberry lollipops are superior to believing that lemon lollipops are superior, nothing about your experience changes. It doesn't feel any different to have the one belief rather than the other.

Perceptual states are not alone among mental states in being qualitative – emotions, moods, and sensations also have a phenomenal feel. The experiences of having an itch or a pain both have phenomenal feels, and what it's like to have a persistent itch on your scalp is typically different from what it's like to have a stinging pain on your scalp. That's not to say that we are always able to easily tell the difference between phenomenal states or that we are always very good at identifying which phenomenal feel goes with which type of experience, and in fact, many experiences have phenomenal feels that are very similar to one another. The qualitative character of the experience of seeing a cherry lollipop might be nearly indistinguishable from the qualitative character of the experience of seeing a strawberry lollipop. Likewise, a butterflies-in-one's-stomach feeling might correspond to fear, nervousness, or nausea, and at various times we might not know for sure which of the states we're in.

OTHER MENTAL STATES

At this point, we've canvassed the major categories of mental states that are typically recognized by philosophers. That said, our inventory is not fully exhaustive. In addition to the propositional attitudes that we've considered, as well as emotions, sensations, and perceptual experiences, there are various other mental states that might be harder to categorize. What should we say about imagination and memory? These mental states sometimes seem to take the form of propositional attitudes like belief (as when you imagine that the current heat wave will end soon or remember that there was a worse heat wave last summer) and sometimes seem to take the form of perceptual experiences like illusion or hallucination (as when you imagine a swimming pool or remember swimming in the Pacific Ocean). One might also wonder about mental characteristics that are not best described as states. Consider character traits, such as honesty or patience. Or consider inclinations, such as your inclination to prefer coffee to tea, but to prefer tea to orange juice. With a little effort, you can probably come up with some other examples of mental phenomena that we haven't covered. Nonetheless, the discussion here should provide a solid framework for understanding the kinds of things that philosophers are talking about when they talk about mental states. When theorizing about the mind, these are the kinds of things for which a theory needs to account.

HOW PHILOSOPHERS STUDY THE MIND

The reflections of the previous section were largely taxonomical in nature. We attempted to provide a rough taxonomy of the mind, classifying mental states into different categories, identifying key features, similarities, differences, and so on. But for those readers unfamiliar with philosophy, the way that we arrived at this taxonomy might have seemed somewhat peculiar. When botanists or zoologists want to provide a taxonomy of some particular group of flora or fauna, they'll likely start by going out into the field, armed with binoculars, cameras, and scientific equipment. They'll make observations, collect samples, and return to the lab to conduct an analysis. But our taxonomical investigation in the previous section didn't involve any photos or specimen containers, we didn't go out into the field, and we didn't conduct any laboratory analysis. Rather, our inquiry proceeded largely by way of **introspection**.

INTROSPECTION

Derived from the Latin *spicere* meaning "to look" and *intra* meaning "within," the term "introspection" literally means "looking within." It's by this method of metaphorically looking within that each of us can come to know our own mental states. Moreover, introspection gives us this knowledge in a distinctively first-personal way. Compare the way that you come to know that you yourself have a toothache with the way you come to know that someone else – say your brother – has a toothache. You come to know that your brother has a toothache by observing his behavior, by listening to what he says and does. You might see him grimace, rub the side of his face, take some pain medication, and so on. You might overhear him phoning the dentist to schedule an appointment. Or he might come straight out and tell you that he has a toothache. But you don't need to do any of this to come to know that you yourself have a toothache. Rather, you come to know this simply by feeling the toothache.

Philosophy is often viewed as something of an armchair discipline. Biologists and chemists do their research in the lab, anthropologists do their research in the field, historians do their research in the archives. In contrast, philosophical inquiry is often a matter of conceptual investigation, and as such, it seems that philosophy can be done from the comfort of one's own armchair. There's no need to travel or to get one's hands dirty to conduct a philosophical investigation. This may seem especially true in philosophy of mind, where philosophers have historically relied heavily on introspective exploration in the course of developing their theories.

Some philosophers have worried that introspective methods are unreliable and that they have often led us astray. When a scientist conducts an experiment in a lab or a social scientist conducts a research study, other scientists and social scientists can test that result by attempting to replicate the findings. When it comes to introspection, however, there seems to be no way to test the results. You cannot access my mental states by introspection, nor do you have any way to tell whether I'm a careful and reliable introspector or a careless and unreliable one. At most you can try to introspect your own mental states and see whether you reach similar conclusions. The fact that different philosophers have reached very different conclusions by way of introspection, however, can make the entire introspective method seem suspect.

In an effort to provide a more scientifically rigorous foundation for philosophy, some philosophers in recent years have turned to experimental methods. The methods employed are typically similar to those employed in psychology, from reaction time studies and other kinds of patient studies to statistical analysis, but now they are being employed specifically with an eye towards addressing the kinds of questions that have traditionally been the focus of philosophy. This kind of philosophy – known as **experimental philosophy**, or often just *x-phi* – has become increasingly popular in the first part of the 21st century. With respect to philosophy of mind, experimental philosophers have applied these methods in an effort to shed light on consciousness, the distinction between qualitative and intentional states, and when/how attributions of mentality are appropriate. At this point in time, however, experimental philosophy still remains a minority movement within philosophy of mind.

PHILOSOPHY OF MIND AND THE EMPIRICAL SCIENCES

Even though most philosophers of mind are not themselves engaged in conducting empirical research, it would be a mistake to think of the practitioners in this field as simply engaged in an enterprise of making pronouncements from the armchair. Much contemporary philosophy of mind makes direct contact with relevant scientific and psychological literature, and whatever one's preferred theory of mind, there is a general sense that such theories must take into account our increasing scientific understanding of the workings of the brain if they are going to be at all plausible. Even if philosophers of mind do not conduct empirical research or do laboratory experiments of their own, the best philosophical work takes place against the backdrop of scientific research and experimentation.

Sometimes students coming to the study of philosophy of mind for the first time worry about what philosophy can add to our understanding of mind over and above what we get from cognitive psychology and neuroscience. To some extent, this worry is best addressed by engaging with the theories and issues discussed throughout this book. The proof is in the pudding, so to speak. But to give at least a hint of an answer right from the start, how exactly we are to understand a certain empirical result is rarely a straightforward matter. How empirical results are to be interpreted, and whether and how they support various theories, are often hotly contested matters. Discovering that a certain mental state is associated with activity in a certain region of the brain, for example, does not settle the question of whether that mental state should be identified with that brain activity or should be treated as a causal result of that activity. Even more to the point, many of the questions surrounding the nature of mind do not seem to be straightforwardly empirical matters. Many of the theoretical claims about mind relate not just to what's *actually the case* but also to *what could be the case*, that is, what's *possible*.

THOUGHT EXPERIMENTS

But if we can't learn about what's possible by way of laboratory experiments, how do we learn about it? To address this issue, many philosophers of mind – like philosophers in general – rely on a different kind of experiment in their work. In particular, philosophy of mind is rife with what are commonly referred to as **thought experiments**.

To get a sense of how a thought experiment works, consider the Experience Machine case that was developed by Robert Nozick in the 1970s:

> Suppose there was an experience machine that would give you any experience you desired. Super-duper neuropsychologists could stimulate your brain so that you would think and feel you were writing a great novel, or making a friend, or reading an interesting book. All the time you would be floating in a tank, with electrodes attached to your brain. Should you plug into this machine for life, preprogramming your life experiences?
>
> (Nozick 1974, 42)

Nozick introduces this case in the context of considering the theory of hedonism proposed by English philosopher and jurist Jeremy Bentham. According to hedonism, pleasure (and the avoidance of pain) is the only thing that matters to us. By considering this case, and thinking about whether we would plug into the experience machine, we can explore the plausibility of hedonism. Given that the steady stream of pleasurable experiences produced by the machine means that one would experience more pleasure by plugging in than one would experience by remaining unplugged, any hesitation we feel about plugging in — any sense that we would be missing something if we did so — calls hedonism into question. In this way, Nozick's thought experiment plays an important role in the evaluation of this philosophical theory.

The method of thought experiment plays an important role in many areas of philosophy of mind — in the debate between dualism and physicalism, in the debate about whether computers can have mentality, and so on. Engaging with thought experiments can help reveal a theory's hidden commitments and its unrecognized consequences. It can also shed important light on a theory's advantages and disadvantages. That's not to say that the method is uncontroversial. Some philosophers dismiss them as unreliable, and they worry that when presented with a thought experiment we do not always accurately or completely imagine the scenario with which we have been presented. Moreover, even when philosophers accept the method of thought experimentation as an illuminating one, they may nonetheless find fault with particular thought experiments that have been offered. We will see this dialectic play out at many different points in the discussion of this book.

ARGUMENTS

Our discussion of how philosophers conduct their study of the mind would not be complete, however, without a discussion of logical argumentation. Indeed, a reliance on arguments lies at the heart of virtually all philosophical investigation. In a philosophical context, "argument" should not be seen as synonymous with "fight," and it should not be taken to imply any kind of animosity or anger. Rather, for philosophers, an **argument** is a piece of logical reasoning containing a claim or set of claims offered to support some further claim. The claim being supported is called the **conclusion**, while the reasons offered in support of it are called **premises**.

To see what an argument looks like, we might return to our discussion of Nozick's Experience Machine thought experiment. The thought experiment itself does not show that hedonism is false. Rather, this conclusion is derived from an argument in which the thought experiment is embedded. The argument might go something like this: hedonism claims that the only good is pleasure. But since someone could rationally choose not to plug into the experience machine, even though the experience machine would maximize pleasure, there must be some goods other than pleasure. So hedonism must be false.

In order to elucidate the logical structure of an argument, philosophers often put it in standard form. When an argument is in standard form, the premises are separated from one another and presented in a list form, with the conclusion being the final item on the list. Often this list will include sub-conclusions that are reached along the way. These sub-conclusions are supported by previous premises and are then used in support of subsequent sub-conclusions or the main conclusion. In putting an argument in standard form, philosophers will often list not only premises that are stated explicitly but also premises that are implicit in the piece of reasoning. In standard form, the argument just given looks something like this:

1   If hedonism is true, then there are no goods other than pleasure.
2   One can maximize pleasure by plugging into the experience machine.
3   One can rationally choose not to plug into the experience machine.
4   If one can rationally choose not to plug into the experience machine even though doing so would maximize pleasure, then there must be some goods other than pleasure.
5   Thus, there must be some goods other than pleasure. (From 2,3,4)
6   Thus, hedonism is not true. (From 1,5)

Here, steps 1 through 4 are premises, step 5 is a sub-conclusion, and step 6 is the main conclusion. The parentheticals at the end of steps 5 and 6 indicate which steps they depend on. Some such notation is typically included in standard form for each sub-conclusion or conclusion.

One advantage of putting an argument in standard form is that doing so makes it easier to evaluate. In evaluating arguments, philosophers focus on two different questions: first, do the premises support the conclusion? And second, are the premises true? As this may suggest, the first question is about the *relationship* between premises and conclusion, and we can ask about whether this relationship holds independently of whether the premises are true.

Arguments come in two different types: **inductive** and **deductive**. In inductive arguments, the premises are put forth in an effort to make the truth of the conclusion more probable. When evaluating the relationship between premises and conclusion of an inductive argument we thus want to know whether the premises, if true, would succeed in doing so. When they do, we say that the argument is *inductively strong*. Inductive strength comes in degrees. Arguments where the premises make the conclusion very likely are inductively stronger than arguments where the premises only make the conclusion moderately likely.

In deductive arguments, the premises are put forth in an effort to guarantee the truth of the conclusion. When evaluating the relationship between premises and conclusion of a deductive argument we thus want to know whether the premises, if true, succeed in doing so. When they do, we say that the argument is *deductively valid*, or just *valid*. Validity does not come in degrees; an argument is either valid or invalid. When an argument is valid, it is impossible for the premises to be true while the conclusion is false. When all of the premises of a deductive argument are true, and the argument is also valid, the argument is referred to as being *deductively sound*, or just *sound*.

Most of the arguments that we will discuss during our exploration of philosophy of mind will be deductive arguments. Typically, such arguments will be valid, and so our focus in evaluating them will be on evaluating the truth of the premises. In those cases where we encounter inductive arguments, they will typically have at least a moderate degree of inductive strength. Thus, there too our focus in evaluating the arguments will be on evaluating the truth of the premises. The questions of how to determine an argument's validity or inductive strength fall under the subfield of philosophy known as **logic**.

THEORIES OF MIND: A ROUGH OVERVIEW

When thinking about philosophical theories of mind, it's perhaps simplest to start with the contrast between dualist positions and monist positions.

DUALISM

Dualist philosophers believe that there are two fundamentally different kinds of things in the world – those that are made of matter, i.e., that are material, and those that are not, i.e., that are immaterial. Like trees, tables, and tadpoles, the human body – the head, neck, torso, arms, hands, legs and feet, plus all the organ systems that it contains – is a material object. In contrast, the dualist claims that the human mind is not a material object. It is not made up of matter. Historically, many philosophers such as Plato and Aquinas offered versions of a dualist position, but the view is most closely associated with Descartes. In his *Meditations on First Philosophy*, published in the mid-17th century, Descartes offered a sustained development and defense of the view that has since become widely influential. In contemporary versions of the view, the contrast between the two kinds of existing things is often put not in terms of materiality vs. immateriality but in terms of physical vs. non-physical, or physical vs. mental.

MONISM: IDEALISM, MATERIALISM, AND RUSSELLIAN MONISM

In contrast to the dualists, **monist** philosophers believe that there is one fundamental kind of thing in the world. Monists thus divide primarily into two main sub-groups – those who believe that everything that exists is immaterial, and those who believe that everything that exists is material. Philosophers in the first sub-group have been referred to as **idealists**, and historically this position was most closely associated with George Berkeley, an 18th-century Irish philosopher. In fact Berkeley was both an idealist – believing that everything that exists either is a mind or depends on a mind for its existence – and an immaterialist – believing that no material objects exist. These views can be jointly summarized by his famous motto *esse est percipi*, that is, to be is to be perceived.

Philosophers in the second sub-group have been referred to as **materialists**, and historically this position was most closely associated with Thomas Hobbes, a 17th-century English philosopher. According to Hobbes, everything that exists is really just matter in motion. Thus, the mind too can be nothing more than matter in motion. As our scientific understanding of the world has developed over the past several hundred years, it's become clear that many of the things that exist and that are studied by science – electromagnetic forces, gravitational fields, bosons, and so on – are not accurately described as being made of matter. Thus, contemporary versions of the materialist view are typically referred to as **physicalism** rather than materialism, and the view is now usually summarized as the claim that everything that exists is physical rather than as the claim that everything that exists is a material object.

In the late 19th and early 20th century, a third kind of monist position was advanced, one that's become known as **Russellian monism**. According to Russellian monists such as William James and Bertrand Russell, all reality is ultimately composed of one fundamental kind of thing, but what we find at the level of ultimate reality is not accurately described as either the idealists or the materialists traditionally described it. Rather, as Russell puts in *The Analysis of Mind*:

> The stuff of which the world of our experience is composed is, in my belief, neither mind nor matter, but something more primitive than either. Both mind and matter seem to be composite, and the stuff of which they are compounded lies in a sense between the two, in a sense above them both, like a common ancestor.
>
> (Russell 1921, 10–11)

THE CONTEMPORARY DEBATE

In an effort to provide the overall lay of the land and provide some historical context, I began this section by contrasting dualism with monism. But in essence, contemporary philosophy of mind – and it's the contemporary debate that we'll really be focusing on in what follows – is best cast as a contrast between dualism and physicalism. One might see the basic question driving the debate about the mind-body problem as something like the following: can our mental life be explained entirely in terms of the brain (and the larger neural system)? While the physicalist answers in the affirmative, the dualist answers in the negative. For the dualist, a neural explanation does not tell the entire story but rather leaves something out.

WHAT LIES AHEAD

In the next three chapters, we will explore these two theories at greater length. In Chapter Two, we take an in-depth look at dualism, whereas in Chapter Three, we take an in-depth look at physicalism. In Chapter Four, we turn to a third theory that has been highly influential in contemporary philosophy of mind, namely, *functionalism*. According to functionalism, we can best explain the mind not in terms of the brain's physical make-up but rather in terms of its functional organization. Mental states are best understood not as physical states but as functional states. Functionalism is sometimes motivated by a computational analogy: the mind:brain relationship is like the software:hardware relationship. As we will see, it's difficult to situate the functionalist theory with respect to the dualist-physicalist dichotomy; it does not fit neatly into either category. Though most functionalists are physicalists, there is an important sense in which the theory is compatible with dualism.

The computational analogy underlying functionalism prompts an interesting question: if what matters for mentality is that a system is running a certain kind of program, then might it not be the case that things other than humans – in particular, non-organic things like machines – could run the relevant program? In Chapter Five we take up this question at length by way of an exploration of the possibility of machine mentality. Can machines have mental states, and if so, what kinds? How would we know if they did?

Finally, in Chapter Six, we look ahead and take up issues concerning the future of the mind – and thus the future of philosophy of mind. As technology continues to advance at a remarkable rate, not only are we seeing the creation of machines that might seem to have mentality, but we are also seeing the advent of technologies that impact our own mental lives and capacities – from smartphones to cloud storage to nanobots. In this final chapter, we explore how such technologies have affected and likely will continue to influence our conception of mind and mentality. In the course of doing so, we also take up questions about whether (and, if so, to what extent) the mind might extend beyond the boundaries of skull and skin.

CONCLUDING SUMMARY

The goal of this beginning chapter was to introduce readers to the philosophical study of mind and to lay the groundwork for the subsequent discussion of the book. To do this, we started with a whirlwind tour of the mind that allowed us to inventory the kinds of states that philosophers talk about when they talk about mental states. Next we discussed the methodologies that philosophers employ when studying the mind. Since these methods are frequently used in other philosophical subfields, this section of the chapter has the added benefit of having introduced philosophical methodology more broadly. The third main section of the chapter provided an overview of the different theories that philosophers have put forward in attempting to account for the nature of mind, theories that we will encounter in more detail throughout the book. Finally, the chapter closed with a very brief overview of the contents of the book.

FURTHER READING

For an introduction to philosophical theorizing about introspection, see my article in the *Internet Encyclopedia of Philosophy* available at https://www.iep. utm.edu/introspe/. One influential recent criticism of the reliability of introspection can be found in Eric Schwitzgebel's "The Unreliability of Naïve Introspection," *The Philosophical Review* 117: 245–273 (2008). Tim Bayne responds to this critique in "Introspective Insecurity" (2015), available online at https://open-mind.net/DOI?isbn=9783958570214.

For an extended discussion of thought experiments and their role in philosophy, see Sorensen 1992, especially Ch. 4. For some reasons to be skeptical about thought experiments, see Wilkes (1988), pp. 1–21.

There are many good logic textbooks available that discuss both deductive and inductive arguments. The textbook *for all x* by P.D. Magnus and Jonathan Ichikawa is available freely online, open access, at https://philpap ers.org/archive/MAGFXU.pdf; the first chapter provides a useful introduction to the evaluation of arguments.

DUALISM

In Terry Bisson's "Meat," a short story that was originally published in *Omni* but that has subsequently been widely circulated on the internet, two intelligent aliens capable of faster-than-light travel discuss a race of sentient creatures that they have recently encountered in their exploration of the universe. Throughout the short story, which consists entirely of dialogue, one of these two aliens tries to explain to the other what's been discovered about this new race: though they are indeed sentient – though they think and feel – they are made entirely of meat. The second alien is incredulous. At one point, for example, they have the following exchange:

> "No brain?"
> "Oh, there's a brain all right. It's just that the brain is made out of meat! That's what I've been trying to tell you."
> "So ... what does the thinking?"
> "You're not understanding, are you? You're refusing to deal with what I'm telling you. The brain does the thinking. The meat."
> "Thinking meat! You're asking me to believe in thinking meat!"
> "Yes, thinking meat! Conscious meat! Loving meat. Dreaming meat. The meat is the whole deal! Are you beginning to get the picture or do I have to start all over?"
>
> (Bisson 1991)

Though the creatures and the planet on which they live go unnamed in the story, Bisson's descriptions make it exceedingly likely that the aliens have happened upon Earth and that we humans are the subject of the discussion.

Are we humans made entirely of meat? In a sense, it's this question that underlies the divide between **dualist** and **physicalist** views. Like the second alien, dualists reject the idea that meat alone can think, be conscious, fall in love, and so on. In their view, there must be something more than just a "meat"-like brain to account for our mentality.

Why might someone think this? Here's a quick thought experiment, based loosely on some remarks from 17th-century philosopher Gottfried Leibniz that might help to motivate the view. Suppose that someone has invented a piece of technology that enables its user to become very, very tiny — as small as Ant-Man can get, say. Next suppose someone shrinks herself and starts exploring inside another person's skull and all the way into that person's brain. As this shrunken traveler moves about, she'll see neurons, axons, and basal ganglia, but no matter how hard she looks she'll never see thoughts. She'll never see any emotions or beliefs or hopes or dreams. She'll never see any consciousness. Since she's seen all there is to see about the brain, and since she can't find the mental stuff anywhere, it seems natural to conclude that this mental stuff must be something over and above the brain, something different from it. In other words, dualism starts to seem like a very attractive option.

In this chapter, we will explore the dualist view. In the first half of the chapter, we undertake an exploration of the version of dualism developed by 17th-century French philosopher René Descartes. This view is often referred to as *Cartesian dualism* ("Cartesian" being the adjectival form of the name "Descartes"). In the second half of the chapter, we turn to contemporary versions of the view.

CARTESIAN DUALISM

Though Descartes develops and defends his dualist view in many different works, we will here focus on the view as it is laid out in his *Meditations on First Philosophy*, a work written in Latin that was originally published in 1641. In these Meditations, of which there are six, Descartes addresses several different topics in addition to the nature of the mind. Perhaps most notably, the First Meditation lays the groundwork for what's become known as a *foundationalist epistemology*, i.e., the view that all human knowledge ultimately rests on certain bedrock principles that can themselves be known independently of any experience of the world. Also notable are the two arguments that he offers for the existence of God, one in the Third Meditation and one in the Fifth Meditation.

The Second and the Sixth Meditation are of most importance with respect to the development of Cartesian dualism. Over the course of these two meditations, we get a detailed development of the view itself as well as three distinct arguments in support of it. Though Descartes himself does not name them, we'll refer to them as *The Argument from Doubt, The Conceivability Argument*, and *The Divisibility Argument*.

As will become clear from our discussion of these arguments, Descartes thinks of the mind as an entity or a thing. In his view, it is not a physical entity. It is an entity that exists outside of space. But it is still an entity in its own right and, moreover, one that is capable of independent existence. In his terms, it is a *substance*. For this reason, his view is often referred to as **substance dualism**. This aspect of dualism has been largely abandoned by contemporary dualists, who tend not to see the mind as a substance. Rather than claiming there are two fundamentally different kinds of substances in the world, these contemporary dualists claim that there are two fundamentally different kinds of properties in the world. For this reason, the view is often referred to as **property dualism**. On the property dualist view, although all of the substances that exist are physical substances, some physical substances like the brain have both physical and mental properties. But more on that later in the chapter, after we have discussed Cartesian dualism itself.

THE ARGUMENT FROM DOUBT

To explain the Argument from Doubt, which is offered at the start of the Second Meditation, it will be helpful first to provide a little context. In the First Meditation, Descartes begins by attempting to provide a solid foundation for the knowledge that's to come as a result of his philosophical inquiry. In order to do this, he believes that he must first free himself from all of his prior opinions that are uncertain, that is, he has to get rid of all of his beliefs where there is room for doubt. Ultimately, by considering the possibility that he is being deceived by an all-powerful evil demon, Descartes realizes that almost nothing that he believes can be held with certainty – indeed, that he can't even be sure of the existence of the world around him.

At the start of the Second Meditation, Descartes worries that the skeptical conclusions reached in the prior Meditation may imply that he can't even be sure of his own existence. But he quickly retracts that conclusion, realizing that the very possibility of deception by an evil demon requires him to exist in order to be deceived. In a very famous passage, Descartes notes that "this proposition, *I am, I exist*, is necessarily true whenever it is put forward by me or conceived in my mind." Summarizing this passage with the phrase "I think, therefore I am," philosophers often refer to it as the *Cogito*. ("I think, therefore I am" is a translation of the Latin *cogito ergo sum*.)

The Cogito leads directly into the Argument from Doubt. For as Descartes notes, though he can doubt the existence of his body, he cannot doubt the existence of himself, that is, of a thinking thing, a mind. This difference seems to show that the mind is a different thing from the body. Putting this reasoning in standard argument form, as discussed in Chapter One, we get:

The Argument from Doubt:

1   I (Descartes) cannot doubt the existence of my mind.
2   Thus, my mind has the property that I (Descartes) cannot doubt its existence.
3   I (Descartes) can doubt the existence of my body.
4   Thus, my body has the property that I (Descartes) can doubt its existence.
5   If my mind and my body differ with respect to their properties, then my mind is a different thing from my body.
6   Thus, my mind is a different thing from my body. [From 2,4,5]

ASSESSING THE ARGUMENT FROM DOUBT

Initially, this argument may seem to utilize an effective argumentative strategy. One good way to try to prove that two individuals or things are different from one another is to find a property that one has that the other lacks. Suppose, for example, that we were trying to figure out Superman's secret identity. Since Superman is 6'3" tall, while Gotham City billionaire Bruce Wayne is 6'2" tall, it seems that we can conclude that Bruce Wayne is not Superman.

This strategy for distinguishing two individuals or things, represented in premise 5 of the argument, utilizes a principle called **Leibniz' Law**, named after the German philosopher Gottfried Leibniz. According to this principle, if two things A and B are identical to one another, then they share all their properties in common. This point is sometimes put by saying that identical things are indiscernible from one another. (For this reason, Leibniz' Law is sometimes referred to as the *principle of the indiscernibility of identicals*.) Since Superman and Bruce Wayne do not share all their properties – they differ in height – they cannot be identical to one another. Since the mind and the body do not share all of their properties – they differ with respect to dubitability, i.e., whether their existence can be doubted – it looks like we can likewise conclude that they cannot be identical to one another.

Unfortunately, however, closer examination reveals that the Argument from Doubt goes astray in its implementation of Leibniz' Law. The problem is that dubitability seems an importantly different kind of property from height. Consider Lois Lane for a moment. Lois Lane knows full well that Superman is a superhero. This isn't something she doubts. But she does doubt that Clark Kent, the mild-mannered reporter for *The Daily Planet*, is a superhero. Does this show that Superman is not Clark Kent? Surely not. The problem is that dubitability isn't really a genuine property of Superman or Clark Kent. It's not a property that they have in and of themselves but rather only an observer-relative one. Whether they have or lack this property is relative to Lois Lane. Likewise, the dubitability in the Argument from Doubt is also observer-relative. Descartes' mind and his body neither have nor lack the property of dubitability in and of themselves, but only relative to Descartes. Ultimately, then, it seems that the Argument from Doubt is unsuccessful.

THE CONCEIVABILITY ARGUMENT

Descartes returns to the question of the relationship between the mind and the body in the Sixth Meditation, a meditation that is subtitled "The existence of material things and the real distinction between mind and body." To establish that there is this distinction, that is, to establish that dualism is correct, Descartes relies principally on the fact we can conceive of the mind and body as existing apart from one another – or as he puts it, that we can clearly and distinctly understand the mind apart from the body. Why does this fact about what we can conceive show anything about the mind and the body themselves? For Descartes, the answer involves God:

> Everything which I clearly and distinctly understand is capable of being created by God so as to correspond exactly with my understanding of it. Hence the fact that I can clearly and distinctly understand one thing apart from another is enough to make me certain that the two things are distinct, since they are capable of being separated, at least by God.

At this point in the *Meditations*, Descartes believes that he has proved the existence of God – in fact he believes he has done this twice over! – and so he feels entitled to rely on God in offering his argument for dualism. For those who do not share Descartes' confidence in the success of those arguments, his reliance on them will here be problematic. Fortunately, the basic principles underlying Descartes' argument for dualism do not crucially depend on the existence of God. Since, in general, an argument is strengthened by avoiding reliance on controversial premises, we will here focus on a secularized version of the argument. Putting this argument into standard form, we get:

The Conceivability Argument:

1   Whatever is clearly and distinctly conceivable is possible.
2   I can clearly and distinctly conceive the mind existing without the body.
3   Thus, it is possible for the mind to exist without the body. [From 1,2]
4   If it is possible for A to exist without B, then A and B are distinct entities.
5   Thus, the mind and the body are distinct entities, i.e., dualism is true. [From 3,4]

This argument has two principal stages. In the first stage of the argument, Descartes moves from a claim about what's conceivable to a claim about what's possible. In the second stage of the argument, Descartes moves from a claim about what's possible to a claim about the truth of dualism. As we will see, the real work of the argument occurs in the first stage.

Suppose that you've just moved into a new apartment, and to help you furnish it a friend offers to give you his old couch that he no longer needs. "I'll give it to you for free," he says, "as long as you take responsibility for moving it." The couch is pretty big, and you're not sure whether it will fit in your small SUV or whether you'll have to rent a truck. You don't want to pay for the truck rental unless absolutely necessary, but you also don't want to lug the couch down two flights of stairs only to have to lug it back up again if it doesn't fit in your SUV (you can't leave it outside while you go to the truck rental place). You might take various measurements in an effort to figure things out but what you'll also probably do is engage in an act of imagination: you visualize the couch, visualize the SUV, and mentally rotate the couch this way and that to see whether it is going to fit inside. Via this imaginative act, in other words, you determine whether it is *possible* for the couch to fit into the car.

Though Descartes talks of conceiving rather than of imagining, it's a similar kind of reasoning that's used in the first half of the Conceivability Argument to reach the possibility claim in step 3. From here, the rest of the argument is relatively unproblematic. If it's possible for the mind and the body to exist apart from one another, then even if as a matter fact in actual life they always exist together, they must nonetheless be two separate things. Consider a simple analogy: suppose there is a parasite who invades a host just as they both come into existence. For their entire existence, the parasite and the host exist together, and they both cease to exist at the exact same moment. But since it's possible that things might have been otherwise, since it's possible that the parasite might have died before the host and that the host would have lived on with-out it, we can conclude that the host and the parasite are distinct entities. The mere possibility of their separate existence is enough to show that they are distinct things.

The Conceivability Argument sometimes rubs people the wrong way. The worry is usually something like this: how can we conclude something about how things are in reality simply on the basis of what we can conceive? The fact that I can conceive of a tiger hiding in my garage does not entitle me to conclude that there is a tiger in my garage! What makes Descartes' reasoning any different from this?

Here's an analogy that might help to show why the reasoning employed by the Conceivability Argument isn't as obviously hopeless as this worry seems to suggest. Consider a glass vase sitting on a shelf fully intact. We can conceive of the vase shattering into lots and lots of pieces were it to be dropped on the floor. From this, you might think, we can conclude that the vase is actually fragile. That's not to say that it is actually *broken*; as we said, it's fully intact. But our act of conceiving might plausibly seem to show us something about a property that it has, namely, its fragility. Likewise, the fact that we can conceive of the mind and the body as existing separately from one another does not show that they are actually separated from one another. But our act of conceiving here too might seem to show us something about a property they have, namely, that they are distinguishable entities. And that's all that the dualist needs to support the claim that the mind and the body are distinct from one another. None of this shows that the Conceivability Argument is successful – that's a question we'll consider in more depth in the next section – but it should help to show that the argument is at least not a complete non-starter.

ASSESSING THE CONCEIVABILITY ARGUMENT

Before publishing the *Meditations*, Descartes circulated a draft manuscript to various of his contemporaries – mainly philosophers and theologians – in an effort to get feedback from them. Selections from this feedback, along with his replies, were included with the published version of the *Meditations*. All in all, there were six sets of objections, and though the authors were not named by Descartes, scholars have been able to identify them with some confidence. Of special interest to us here is the fourth set of objections, generally believed to have been authored by Antoine Arnauld, a French theologian, philosopher, and mathematician. In his remarks on the Conceivability Argument, Arnauld offered an especially incisive objection that presents a significant threat to Descartes' reasoning.

To pose his objection, Arnauld asks the reader to consider a right triangle. As has been mathematically proven, the Pythagorean theorem holds of all right triangles, that is, the sum of the squares of the two shorter sides is equal to the square of the hypotenuse. But now consider someone who has not been well trained in geometry – call him Oliver. Not understanding much about geometric relations, Oliver may well be able to conceive of a right triangle existing for which the Pythagorean theorem does not hold. But is Oliver entitled to conclude from this that it is possible for there to be a right triangle for which the Pythagorean theorem does not hold? Surely not. Likewise, says Arnauld, someone who takes themself to have conceived that the mind can exist without the body is not entitled to conclude that it is possible for the mind to exist without the body. In this way, by questioning whether conceivability implies possibility, Arnauld's objection calls premise 1 into question.

This objection puts considerable pressure on the Conceivability Argument. In an effort to save premise 1, Descartes might note that the premise is intended to be read as imposing a rather strict requirement. One must not simply conceive of something but must conceive of it *clearly and distinctly*. In Oliver's case, though he took himself to have conceived of a right triangle, perhaps he only conceived of something that is *nearly* a right triangle. Or perhaps his conceiving was in some other way confused or muddled. This line of response denies that Oliver's mathematical conceiving meets the strict requirement intended by premise 1 of the Conceivability Argument. Once this strict requirement is correctly understood, Arnauld's alleged counterexample fails.

Though this response might initially look promising, it ultimately proves problematic. In tightening the requirements of premise 1, Descartes may be able to fend off the Oliver case, but in the process of doing so he introduces a different worry for the argument. The problem now becomes premise 2. By inflating the requirement of clear and distinct conception in an effort to reject Arnauld's counterexample, Descartes opens himself up to worries about whether he can clearly and distinctly conceive of the mind without the body. Maybe, like Oliver, Descartes' conceiving is in some way confused or muddled. Given that Oliver cannot himself identify the problem with his act of conceiving, why should Descartes expect that he himself would be able to identify the problem with his act of conceiving?

In this way, Arnauld's objection poses a serious challenge for Descartes' Conceivability Argument. In order to be at all plausible, premise 1 needs to be understood as offering a very strict requirement. But once premise 1 is interpreted in this fashion, premise 2 no longer seems as plausible.

That said, the Conceivability Argument seems to have more potential than the Argument from Doubt, and as we will see, contemporary dualists have revived the argument in various ways. Though there is more to be said about conceivability and its role in the defense of dualism, we will leave this issue for now and return to it in our discussion of contemporary versions of dualism later in this chapter.

THE DIVISIBILITY ARGUMENT

In addition to the Conceivability Argument, the Sixth Meditation also contains a second argument for dualism. This argument has received considerably less scrutiny than the Conceivability Argument, and even Descartes seems to treat it largely as an afterthought. But it is worth at least a brief look.

Descartes offers the argument in the context of thinking more closely about the nature of the body and of its relationship to the mind. As he succinctly writes: "there is a great difference between the mind and the body, inasmuch as the body is by its very nature always divisible, while the mind is utterly indivisible." While the mind is not capable of being divided, the body is. Putting this argument into standard form, we get

The Divisibility Argument:

1 The body is divisible.
2 The mind is not divisible.
3 If the mind and body differ with respect to their properties, then the mind is a different thing from the body.
4 Thus, the mind is a different thing from the body. [From 1,2,3]

Like the Argument from Doubt that we considered earlier, this argument utilizes a Leibniz' Law strategy, with the principle here represented by premise 3. But while the Argument from Doubt relied on dubitability, a property that was observer-relative, the Divisibility Argument relies on divisibility. Since whether an object is divisible is a property the object has in and of itself, independent of any observer, the application of Leibniz' Law is unproblematic. The main question before us, then, is whether the premises are true.

ASSESSING THE DIVISIBILITY ARGUMENT

To determine the truth of the premises of the Divisibility Argument, we need to reflect on the notion of divisibility employed in the argument. Consider an amoeba undergoing fission. When the amoeba divides, it becomes two separate amoebas, each of them complete on its own. The human body is not divisible in this sense. There is no way to divide it in two that results in two separate and complete bodies. But while the body is not divisible *into wholes*, there is another sense in which it is divisible. It is divisible *into parts*. Descartes' claim that the body is divisible in this sense seems plausible. We can partition the body into various separately identifiable entities: the head, the neck, the trunk, the arms and legs, and so on. The brain too is divisible into separately identifiable entities such as the left and right hemispheres, or the cerebral cortex, the cerebellum, and the medulla oblongata.

What about premise 2, the claim that the mind is not divisible? Is it true that the mind cannot be divided into parts? In defending this premise, Descartes considers how one might try to argue that the mind too has parts. In particular, he supposes that one might point to the various faculties of the mind – the faculty of the will, the faculty of understanding, the faculties of sense perception, and so on – as distinct parts. But Descartes does not find this objection very compelling. In his view, it is one and the same mind, the whole mind, that wills, that understands, that perceives, and so on. And any idea or thought or perception that we have is really an idea or thought or perception of the whole mind, not of a part of it. This point is often put by saying that consciousness is *unified*. (We will return to the issue of the unity of consciousness in Chapter Six.) Moreover, faculties like the will or the understanding aren't really distinct parts of the mind the way an arm is a distinct part of the body. Though an arm could continue to exist independently of the body if we were to separate the two, the faculty of the will or the faculty of the understanding can't really continue to exist independently of the mind if we were to try and extract them. In fact, the mere talk of extraction here doesn't really make sense.

But there are other ways that we might divide the mind into parts. For example, we might consider the conscious mind and the unconscious mind as two different parts of it. Alternatively, we might consider cases of dissociative identity disorder (DID). As characterized by the most recent version of the *Diagnostic and Statistical Manual of Mental Disorders*, an individual with DID experiences a "disruption of identity characterized by two or more distinct personality states … The disruption of identity involves marked discontinuity in sense of self and sense of agency…" The different personality states, which used to be referred to as "personalities" but now are more commonly referred to as "alters," tend to have executive control of the body at different times, and an alter often doesn't have any memories of what's happened when it is not in charge of the body. We can think of them as separate streams of consciousness, and perhaps, then, each alter could be considered to be a distinct part of the individual's mind.

Perhaps a deeper objection to premise 2, however, comes from the sense that it begs the question against its opponent, that is, that it presupposes the very point at issue. The reason that we can't seem to think of thoughts, ideas, and perceptions as distinct parts of a substance is that we're already thinking of them as immaterial. The defense of premise 2 seems to presuppose that these mental items are not states of the brain, a physical entity that as we have seen is separable into distinct parts. But if the defense of premise 2 relies on the assumption that the mind is immaterial, then the Argument from Divisibility cannot be used to show that the mind is immaterial, i.e., it cannot be used in support of the dualist view.

INTERACTIONISM

Looking at the arguments that Descartes offered in support of his dualism helps us to understand the basic contours of his view. But it will be worth pausing a moment to talk further about one important aspect of it. As we noted above, and as became clear in our discussion of the arguments that Descartes gives for his view, he treats the mind and body as two distinct substances. But once one makes this claim, a further question then arises. What is the relationship between the mind and the body? In Descartes' view, the relationship is a very close one. As he puts it, the mind and body "form a unit" and are "intermingled" with one another. We don't merely perceive events that happen to our bodies, the way sailors perceive events that happen to their ship, but we directly experience such events.

These observations lead Descartes to what's become known as *interactionism* or *interactionist dualism*, the view that there is two-way causal interaction between mind and body. Events in the mind cause events in the body, as when my desire for something to drink causes me to get up from my chair and walk to the kitchen. Likewise, events in the body cause events in the mind, as when a muscle cramp in my calves causes me to feel pain and to resolve to stay better hydrated.

Importantly, this aspect of Descartes' view forestalls an objection that is often raised against dualism – what we might call the *objection from neuroscientific research*. Though Descartes was himself a respected scientist, the science of his day was significantly impoverished in comparison with the science of the 21st century. In light of contemporary advances in neuroscience, people often point to all that we've learned about brain function and the nervous system as definitive proof against dualism. Take itches, for example. "Look," the objector will say. "We know that itching sensations occur when the pruriceptors of certain specialized nerve cells are activated. We can explain itching sensations solely in terms of this process. So doesn't that show that there isn't a separate mind? It's all about the brain and nervous system."

As should be clear, however, this scientific result is in no way incompatible with Descartes' version of dualism and, in fact, could even be predicted by it. Since Descartes believes that events in the brain will cause events in the mind, he can explain the relevant scientific result in causal terms. While the objector takes the result to show that the mind must wholly consist in the brain, Descartes takes the result to show that the mind is causally affected by the brain. It's hard to see how the scientific results favor one explanation over the other. Perhaps the objector might introduce considerations of simplicity, arguing that their explanation is a simpler one than the explanation offered by Descartes. But whether that's true is not immediately obvious and stands in need of further support. We will return to issues involving considerations of simplicity in Chapter Three when we explore the physicalist view. For now, we will assess interactionism in light of two objections that have been raised against it.

ASSESSING INTERACTIONISM

In the novel *Atonement* by Ian McEwan, one of the characters finds herself mystified by how she manages to control the actions of her body:

> She raised one hand and flexed its fingers and wondered, as she had sometimes before, how this thing, this machine for gripping, this fleshy spider on the end of her arm, came to be hers, entirely at her command. Or did it have some little life of its own? She bent her finger and straightened it. The mystery was in the instant before it moved, the dividing moment between moving and not moving, when her intention took effect. It was like a wave breaking.
>
> (McEwan 2002, 33)

The puzzling nature of mind-body causation is often raised as an objection to Descartes' interactionism. As these considerations were initially raised by Elisabeth, Princess of Bohemia, with whom Descartes had extensive correspondence, we'll call it *Princess Elisabeth's objection*. Given that the mind in Descartes' view is an immaterial substance, it remains completely mysterious how it could causally interact with a material substance like the body. When we think of ordinary instances of causation, as when a cue stick causes a billiard ball to move across the billiards table, or when a rock causes a glass window pane to shatter, we have physical contact between the two entities. The cue stick comes into direct physical contact with the billiard ball, and the rock comes into direct physical contact with the glass window pane. Given that the mind is immaterial, however, it cannot come into direct physical contact with the body. How, then, can there be any causal relations between the two? How can an intention, a wholly mental occurrence, bring it about that a finger moves? Descartes, in answer to Elisabeth, was largely evasive, and it's not clear that he treated this first objection with the seriousness it deserves.

The second objection, one that has become especially prevalent in contemporary philosophy of mind, is what we'll call the objection from *causal closure*. It is a fundamental principle of contemporary scientific inquiry that every physical event can be given a complete explanation in wholly physical terms. Though our ancestors might once have viewed lightning and thunder as having been brought about by the gods as an expression of their wrath, for example, we now can explain them entirely in terms of the motion of electrons, electrical forces, the vibration of air molecules, and so on. The power of physical explanation extends not just to events like lightning and thunder, but also to movements of the body.

Take a case in which you raise your arm. In explaining this action, we might trace the motion back from the muscle fibers ratcheting past one another, to the chemical impulse that was received by the muscle, to the firing of a motor neuron inside the spinal cord. And we can trace the firing of the motor neuron back farther to its having reached a certain threshold of action potential, and so on. Each of these events in the causal chain can be wholly explained by the event that came before them, without invoking anything mental whatsoever. But if your arm raising can be explained entirely in terms of the brain and nervous system, then there doesn't seem to be any work for the mind to do. Your desire to raise your arm, for example, seems entirely superfluous to the explanation. A similar explanatory story can be told for all other bodily movements or events. In the case of some of these movements or events, we may not yet have the complete explanation entirely worked out. But it seems like only a matter of time before such explanations will be completed.

The options available to the dualist in response to the objection from causal closure are not very palatable. The first possible response is a simple one: it consists of denying causal closure. But this pits the dualist against science, and that's not a comfortable place for the dualist to be.

A second possible response to the objection, one that takes contemporary science seriously, attempts to find a place for mental causation alongside physical causation. This response is pursued primarily by invoking considerations from quantum theory. Quantum indeterminacy suggests that, at the quantum level, the physical facts do not always determine specific outcomes. Some interactionist dualists, such as the Nobel Prize-winning neuroscientist and philosopher Sir John Eccles, have suggested that mental processes might fill these causal gaps. While this suggestion may seem tempting, however, it's not clear that it provides for a sufficiently robust account of mental causation. Even if these quantum-level mental interventions could in some way bubble up to make a difference at the macro level, it's hard to see how this would square with the intuitive picture on which macro-level mental states are genuinely responsible for the causation of physical events. Microscopic mental interventions at the quantum level don't seem adequate to make it the case that it was my desire for an apple that caused me to get up from my chair and walk to the kitchen.

A third possible dualist response involves the suggestion that the bodily movement is over-determined. To understand this response, it will be helpful to consider an ordinary example of over-determination. Consider a case drawn from *Mission Impossible: Rogue Nation*. In this movie, the villain Solomon Lane sends three different highly trained snipers to the Vienna Opera House during a performance of the opera *Turandot* in an attempt to assassinate the Austrian Chancellor. They are all meant to fire their weapons at the same moment, when the singers reach a certain note in the score. Though in the actual movie these plans were thwarted by IMF agent Ethan Hunt, let's suppose for a moment that they weren't. When the note is reached, each of the three snipers fires a bullet at the Chancellor. Each of the three bullets is directly on target, striking the Chancellor's heart, and he is instantly killed. Here we have a clear case of over-determination. Each bullet was, on its own, fully sufficient to cause the Chancellor's death. Had only the first sniper's bullet hit, the Chancellor still would have died, and likewise for the second and third snipers' bullets.

In invoking over-determination as a response to the objection from causal closure, the dualist treats the relevant mental events and the brain/body events analogously to the snipers' bullets. Had the relevant mental events (your desire to raise your arm) occurred without any of the brain/bodily events (the various muscular events and neuronal firings), your arm would still have been raised, and likewise if the brain/bodily events had occurred without any of the mental events. But the first of these claims does not seem at all plausible, and the second doesn't really give the dualist what they want. Rather, it makes the mental state superfluous, analogous to an extra, unneeded sniper.

A fourth possible response available to the dualist seems no better. On this response, the dualist simply concedes that the mind lacks causal efficacy. The mind exists, and it is distinct from the body, but it has no causal power whatsoever. This position, known as **epiphenomenalism**, is an alternative to interactionism. Once one claims that the mind lacks causal power, one can no longer claim that there is two-way causal interaction between the mind and the brain. So while adopting this response allows one to hold on to dualism, it does not allow one to hold on to Cartesian dualism. Epiphenomenalists also tend to reject substance dualism for property dualism, to be discussed below.

Epiphenomenalism offers the dualist a way around the objection from causal closure, but it has struck many philosophers as wildly counterintuitive. How can our desires, our intentions, our pains and itches, be entirely causally impotent? Doesn't this essentially reduce us to mere automata? And, once we deprive the mind of any causal power whatsoever, what sense does it make to claim that it really exists? Such questions prove very difficult for the epiphenomenalist to adequately answer.

THE PAIRING PROBLEM

Before leaving Cartesian dualism, it is worth mentioning one more problem – *the pairing problem* – that confronts any version of substance dualism. Though we often speak of a person's mind as being located inside their head, such talk can be only metaphorical for a dualist. After all, in the dualist's view the mind is an immaterial substance and, as such, lacks any spatial location. So how does it get associated with any particular body? What makes my immaterial mind be associated with this particular body, capable of raising this particular arm or moving this particular leg?

Descartes himself thought that the mind and the body interacted through the pineal gland – a very small organ about the size of a grain of rice that is located at the center of the brain, between the two hemispheres. This fact about its location, along with the fact that almost nothing was known about its function at the time

Descartes was writing, led him to identify it as "the seat of the soul." Unfortunately for Descartes, the function of the pineal gland has since been identified: it is an endocrine gland that secretes melatonin and thereby regulates the body's circadian rhythms. But if Descartes had been right about the pineal gland, this would have given him an answer to the pairing problem.

Absent the pineal gland solution, however, it is unclear how the substance dualist can address the pairing problem. It is hard to see what kind of mechanism could successfully bind an immaterial substance to a material substance. But perhaps the problem is not too overly troubling for the dualist, who might argue that our inability to understand the binding mechanism is just a corollary of our inability to understand how an immaterial substance can exist. On this line of response, the dualist denies that the pairing problem should be seen as an additional problem over and above the problem of understanding the nature of an immaterial substance. That said, as we will see when we turn to contemporary dualism, the problem can be avoided altogether by the embrace of property dualism.

CONTEMPORARY VERSIONS OF DUALISM

In a recent article in *Harper's* magazine, journalist Christopher Beha argues as follows:

> If the sciences had made no headway since Descartes in the effort to understand human consciousness, it might be possible to preserve his distinction [between mind and body], but neurologists, psychologists, and cognitive scientists have learned more than enough to convince them that the mind *is* the physical brain, or at least a function of it, and that no additional mental substance or thinking thing exists.
>
> (Beha 2017)

As he goes on to recount, we now understand which parts of the brain are responsible for a variety of things ranging from basic life functions to speech, spatiotemporal coordination, and higher-order reasoning. We also have developed a sophisticated understanding of perception, memory formation, and memory retrieval. Given all of this scientific progress, though one can perhaps understand why Descartes, stuck as he was with the limited 17th-century understanding of the workings of the brain, would adopt dualism, it might be hard to understand how anyone in the 21st century could still hold on to what appears to be a wildly outdated view.

Interestingly, however, though dualism had largely disappeared from serious philosophical discussion for much of the 20th century, it returned to the philosophical scene in the 1980s and 1990s. Much of the renewed interest was driven by reflection on **qualia**, the phenomenal aspects of our mental states discussed in Chapter One. Though science offers us an explanation of various psychological functions, of why things happen the way they do, it does not seem to be able to offer an explanation of why things feel the way they do. This is what contemporary philosopher David Chalmers has referred to as the **Hard Problem of Consciousness** (Chalmers 1995).

In separating the hard problem from other problems that face researchers studying consciousness, Chalmers does not mean to imply that these other problems are easy. But when it comes to issues such as information processing and behavioral control, there is good reason to be optimistic that continuing scientific investigation into the mechanisms of our cognitive system will provide answers. In contrast, when it comes to questions about how the brain gives rise to qualitative experience – why a physical process should be accompanied by one particular qualitative feel rather than another, or indeed, why it should be accompanied by any qualitative feel at all – we are faced a with a mystery that seems virtually unsolvable.

Take pain, for example. The problem of fully explaining the brain processes associated with pain and the role that pain plays in the human system is one that seems within the reach of science. But the problem of accounting for the fact that these brain processes come with that particular *ouchy* feeling – or accounting for the fact that they come with any feeling at all – is one that science does not seem well positioned to answer. The ouchy feeling of pain seems to lie outside the objective realm in which science operates.

Many of the qualia-based considerations that were raised in the late 20th century are best understood as arguments against the physicalist and functionalist views that had dominated in the middle of the century. It's by seeing what these views leave out that one might become tempted to reconsider a dualist view. We will look at most of these arguments in the course of our discussions of physicalism and functionalism in Chapters Three and Four. But in the remainder of this chapter, we will flesh out the contours of the contemporary dualist view, a view that differs in several important ways from the view offered by Descartes, and we will also consider one important dualist argument that has figured heavily in recent philosophical discussion of the mind.

PROPERTY DUALISM

As we saw above, substance dualists like Descartes believe in the existence of an immaterial, nonphysical substance. Such a substance is generally characterized negatively: it is not made of matter, it does not have a spatial location, it is not extended in space, and so on. But we are generally not given any positive characterization of it, and as such, it is a notion shrouded in mystery. In an effort to avoid this mystery, as well as to avoid other problems attendant to the postulation of immaterial substances, property dualists reject the claim that there are fundamentally two different kinds of substances in the world. There is no thing, the mind, over and above the physical brain. Instead, property dualists claim that there are fundamentally two different kinds of properties in the world. Though some physical things, like rocks, have only physical properties, there are some physical things, like brains, that have both physical and non-physical properties. Included among the brain's physical properties are its weight, size, neuronal structure, and so on. So, for example, some particular brain might have the physical property of weighing 1325 grams. Included among the brain's non-physical properties are its mental states. So, for example, some particular brain might have the mental property of desiring a mug of hot chocolate.

THE ZOMBIE ARGUMENT

More than a decade before American viewers became riveted to their television screens by the zombies populating the world of *The Walking Dead*, zombies started taking center stage in philosophy of mind. But unlike the zombies from this popular television series, or from Hollywood productions ranging from *Night of the Living Dead* to *Zombieland*, philosophical zombies are very much alive – or at least, they would be were they to exist. As philosophers use the term, a **zombie** is a creature who is physically and behaviorally indistinguishable from a human being. The zombie is identical to its human twin at the microphysical level. Unlike its human twin, however, zombies are completely devoid of phenomenal consciousness. They do not have any states with qualitative aspects. That's not to say that they don't act as if they have phenomenal consciousness. They behave as if they are in pain when you stick them with a pin, and they will report that they are in pain – after all, the zombie behaves in ways indistinguishable from its human twin – but they don't experience any painful sensations.

Many philosophers have recently claimed that we can coherently conceive of or imagine the existence of zombies. Utilizing a conceivability-style argument that is reminiscent of the one offered by Descartes, such philosophers move from this claim about the conceivability of zombies to a claim about the possibility of zombies, a claim that in turn is taken to imply some form of dualism (or perhaps some other kind of non-physicalistic **monism**). The zombies, after all, are by definition exactly like us physically. But if two creatures alike physically can differ with respect to consciousness, then it seems to show that consciousness is something over and above the physical.

Putting this argument in standard form, we get the following:

The Zombie Argument:

1   Zombies, creatures that are microphysically identical to conscious beings but that lack consciousness entirely, are conceivable.
2   If zombies are conceivable then they are possible.
3   Therefore, zombies are possible. [From 1,2]
4   If zombies are possible, then consciousness is non-physical.
5   Therefore, consciousness is non-physical. [From 3,4]

Before we move on to evaluating the argument, one important clarification is needed. In particular, we need to discuss the notion of possibility that is employed by the argument. When dualist philosophers claim that zombies are possible, they are here relying on a notion of *logical possibility*, not *physical* or *empirical possibility*. For something to be physically possible, it must be compatible with the laws of physics. For something to be logically possible, though it need not be compatible with the laws of physics, it must be compatible with the laws of logic. So, for example, building a spaceship that travels faster than the speed of light is something that is physically impossible. But building such a spaceship is logically possible. There is nothing incoherent or contradictory about the notion. In contrast, there is something incoherent or contradictory about the existence of a three-dimensional object that is both wholly red and wholly green, or wholly cubical and wholly spherical. Such objects are not only physically impossible but also logically impossible.

In claiming that zombies are possible, then, the dualist is claiming that there is nothing incoherent or contradictory about them. Perhaps they could not exist in our universe, or in any universe that has physical laws like ours – just like there could not be travel faster than the speed of light in our universe or in any universe that has physical laws like ours. But, says the dualist, there is nothing in the postulation of zombies that rules them out on logical grounds.

Like Descartes' Conceivability Argument, the Zombie Argument proceeds in two stages. In the first stage, we move from a claim about the conceivability of zombies to a claim about the possibility of zombies. Our brief reflections above suggest why this move might be plausible: since logical possibility has to do with a certain kind of coherence, there is a tight connection between conceivability and logical possibility. In the second stage, we move from the claim about the possibility of zombies to a claim about the nature of consciousness. How can this move be motivated?

Here it may be helpful to consider an analogy. Suppose that a counterfeiter manages to produce a perfect replica of a twenty-dollar bill. In size, shape, color and so on, the counterfeit bill is exactly like a genuine twenty-dollar bill. They are exactly similar to one another in every physical way. But is the counterfeit bill a piece of United States currency? Is it worth twenty dollars? Here the answer is no. The counterfeiter might get away with using it for purchases, but to be a piece of United States currency, to be worth twenty dollars, the bill has to have been produced by the United States Treasury. If it was made in a dark and dingy basement somewhere, then it doesn't have the same monetary value as the genuine bill. As this suggests, monetary value doesn't depend wholly on the physical properties of the bill itself. It depends on other factors, like where it was produced, and so on. And we could draw this conclusion even if no counterfeiter has ever actually managed to create such a perfect replica. The mere possibility of such a perfect replica is enough to show us something about what monetary value is and what it is not.

Likewise, if we have two beings that are exactly similar to each other in every way, that are physically indistinguishable, and one of them is conscious and one of them is not, we can draw the conclusion that consciousness doesn't depend wholly on the physical properties of the beings themselves. Rather, it must depend on some other factors. And again, we could draw this conclusion even if no zombie duplicate has ever actually existed. The mere possibility of such a zombie duplicate is enough to show us something about what consciousness is and what it is not.

ASSESSING THE ZOMBIE ARGUMENT

In responding to this argument, non-dualist philosophers have tended to pursue three different lines of objection. Some philosophers have questioned whether zombies are really conceivable. Others grant that zombies are conceivable but deny that it is appropriate to move from a claim about their conceivability to a claim about their possibility. Yet others grant that zombies are possible creatures but deny that this shows anything about the nature of consciousness.

Because objections of the second and third type tend to require mastery of a complicated metaphysical apparatus that is not well suited for beginning philosophers of mind, we will here focus primarily on the first type of objection just distinguished. In objecting to premise 1, many philosophers take a similar strategy to the one that we saw Arnauld use against Descartes. In brief, such philosophers argue that we are mistaken to think that we are really conceiving of what we think we are. Perhaps we are conceiving of creatures that are simply very, very similar physically to their human twins, rather than identical to them. After all, in conceiving of the zombie, we are clearly unable to conceive of all of the billions of neurons in the human brain in any detail. Or perhaps the situation that we are conceiving has been misdescribed in some other important way. As argued by Daniel Dennett (1995), a contemporary American

philosopher who has been persistent critic of dualism, "when philosophers claim the zombies are conceivable, they invariably under-
estimate the task of conception (or imagination), and end up
imagining something that violates their own definition."

Chalmers, who is generally credited with bringing the Zombie
Argument to prominence, addresses these concerns directly in his
influential book *The Conscious Mind* (Chalmers 1996). One of
his principal strategies is to try to shift the burden of proof to his
opponent. In denying that zombies are conceivable, it is not enough
for the opponent to note that there might be a hidden conceptual
confusion lurking somewhere in the background. The opponent
needs to give us some sense of what the conceptual confusion is.

But, as Chalmers also notes, there are ways that the defender of
premise 1 can help to bolster their case. In particular, the more they
can do to help show why zombies should be conceivable, the stronger their argument will be. For example, opponents of premise 1
might find themselves having trouble conceiving the sort of complex
and subtle behavior produced by conscious humans being produced
by non-conscious zombies. To help the opponent overcome this
worry, the defender of premise 1 might consider sophisticated robots.
Many people find it easy to conceive of human-like robots that are
wholly mechanical rather than organic. Many people also find it easy
to conceive of such robots as engaging in complex and subtle behavior – behavior that is so complex and subtle that we may even be
fooled into thinking that the robot was human. But such people often
have trouble conceiving of the mechanical robot as having qualitative
mental states. Sure, it can behave as if it is in pain, but it doesn't really
feel the ouchiness; sure it can behave as if it is in love, but it doesn't
really feel the pull on its mechanical heartstrings. (We will return to
these issues in Chapters Four and Five.) If complex and subtle behavior can come apart from qualitative experience in the robot case,
then why couldn't it come apart from qualitative experience in the
zombie case? Insofar as one doesn't see any conceptual incoherence in
the robot case, it's hard to see why there should be any conceptual
incoherence in the zombie case.

As mentioned above, the denial of the conceivability of zombies is
not the only kind of objection that non-dualist philosophers have
brought against the zombie argument. Thus, even if dualists can adequately address this objection, that does not show that the argument is a

successful one. At the present time, it is fair to say that the debate about the zombie argument is both hotly contested and still ongoing.

CONCLUDING SUMMARY

This chapter has introduced us to the dualist view and several of the main arguments that have been offered in support of it, both historically and in the contemporary period. As we have seen, several of these arguments seem pretty problematic, and deep questions can be raised about all of them. Why, then, does the dualist position still play such a central role in contemporary philosophy of mind? Why are so many contemporary philosophers inclined towards the dualist view? Though dualism is most definitely a minority position, surveys have suggested that the view still enjoys considerable support. For example, in a survey conducted in 2009 of over 900 philosophy professors at leading universities throughout the world, though more than half of those surveyed (56.5%) claimed that they accepted or leaned toward physicalism, another quarter of those surveyed (27.1%) indicated support for some sort of non-physicalist alternative like dualism. (The remainder fell into the "Other" category; they were undecided, thought the question is too unclear to answer, accepted an intermediate/alternative view, and so on.)

To a large extent, the benefits of dualism can be appreciated only once one has considered the other available views and the problems that such views face. Though this chapter has surveyed the leading arguments put forth *in support* of dualism, we have not yet explored the arguments put forth *against* physicalist alternatives – and it's in large part because of these anti-physicalist arguments that dualism continues to be a viable alternative. It's thus worth reserving judgment on the viability of dualism at least until we've reviewed those arguments in the next few chapters.

FURTHER READING

The "shrunken traveler" thought experiment described at the beginning of this chapter is inspired by some remarks by Leibniz (often referred to as the mill argument); see especially section 17 of his *Monadology*. See Descartes (1641/1986) for his defense of dualism. Arnauld's criticism of the Conceivability Argument is included in this edition among the selections from the objections. Princess Elisabeth's objection to Descartes' interactionism can be found in Shapiro (2007). For a recent defense of dualism that offers a different version of the conceivability argument, see Gertler (2007). A helpful discussion of the general strategy underlying conceivability arguments can be found in Gendler and Hawthorne (2002). For a discussion of the Divisibility Argument, see Brook and Stainton (2000), Chapter 5.

For an accessible discussion of David Chalmers' hard problem of consciousness, see his "Puzzle of Conscious Experience," in the December 1995 issue of *Scientific American*. The hard problem is discussed in more detail in his book *The Conscious Mind* (1996). The book also contains a detailed treatment of his zombie argument. Daniel Dennett's criticisms of philosophical reliance on zombies can be found in his essay, "The Unimagined Preposterousness of Zombies" in *Brainchildren: Essays on Designing Minds* (Cambridge, MA: MIT Press, 1998).

John Eccles defends an interactionist view in "Brain and Mind, Two or One?" in *Mindwaves: Thoughts on Intelligence, Identity, and Consciousness* (1987). Chalmers, in Chapter 4 of *The Conscious Mind*, defends a version of epiphenomenalism.

The survey results mentioned in the concluding remarks are available online at https://philpapers.org/surveys/.

PHYSICALISM

In antiquity, Democritus understood the soul as a sort of fire, made out of spherical atoms, and he took thought to consist in the physical movement of atoms. In the 17th century, Hobbes claimed that sensations are simply internal motions of the sense organs. But it was not until the 20th century that physicalism – the theory that everything is physical, and hence that all of mentality is physical – became the dominant theory in philosophy of mind. In this chapter, we will explore the physicalist view. We start with a discussion of some of the general motivations lying behind it. We then turn to consideration of specific versions of physicalism, and the relative advantages and disadvantages of such views. After reviewing these targeted criticisms, we turn to some considerations that have been offered against physicalism in general, regardless of the particular version it takes. Many of these criticisms rely on the basic thought that physicalism leaves us unable to explain mental states and qualitative experiences.

GENERAL MOTIVATIONS FOR PHYSICALISM

In order to best present the case for physicalism, it will be worth first saying just a bit more about the theory itself. As we have noted, the physicalists believe that everything that exists is physical. But this claim does not commit them to the claim that the mental does not exist. Rather, they typically accept the claim that there are such things as mental states but go on to deny that these mental states are distinct from physical states. Sometimes this is expressed by saying the mental is *nothing over and above* the physical or that the mental *depends* on the physical. Sometimes this is expressed by invoking the technical notion of **supervenience**.

We can elucidate the notion of supervenience by considering two artworks that are identical all the way down to the microscopic level. The two artworks are the same with respect to shape, size, arrangement of colors, and so on. Now let's ask: are they also the same with respect to beauty? Can one of these two works of art be beautiful while the other is not? Insofar as we're inclined to think that this is a possibility, then we'd be denying that beauty supervenes on properties such as shape, size, and so on. Even if all of those properties are the same, there can still be a difference in beauty. Insofar as we're inclined to deny that this is a possibility, then we're likely to be thinking that beauty supervenes on these properties. Absent a difference in shape, size, color arrangement, and so on, there cannot be a difference in beauty. More generally, when some property A supervenes on property B, it follows that there cannot be a difference with respect to A without their being a difference with respect to B.

It's now easy to see how this framework can be applied to physicalism. A definition of physicalism in terms of supervenience commits the physicalist to the claim that there is no mental difference without a physical difference. If we have two different worlds that are completely identical with respect to all of their physical properties, then those two worlds are completely identical with respect to all of their mental properties. (And, actually, since the physicalist claims that *everything* is physical, not just that the mental is physical, the physicalist will also claim that those worlds are completely identical with respect to all of their properties.) Note that this is something the dualist denies. Recall the philosophical zombies discussed in Chapter Two. My zombie and I are completely identical with respect to all of our physical properties, but we differ with respect to our mental properties. I have phenomenal consciousness, while my zombie twin does not. Acceptance of the possibility of zombies commits the dualist to the denial of supervenience.

An understanding of physicalism in terms of supervenience is often described as *minimal physicalism*, since it is often thought that a commitment to supervenience is required for a view to count as physicalist: Though different versions of physicalism may differ from one another in all sorts of respects, they must share a commitment to the supervenience of the mental on the physical. There is considerably more disagreement about whether supervenience is sufficient for physicalism, but we will not pursue this disagreement here. (For discussion, see Stoljar 2015.) Instead, we'll now turn to consider the case that can be made in favor of the physicalist view.

THE CASE FOR PHYSICALISM

Interestingly, the case for physicalism is often pursued not by presenting positive arguments for the view but instead by showing that its chief rival, dualism, is untenable. For example, in his famous paper "Sensations and Brain Processes," physicalist J.J.C. Smart (1959) identifies his project as "to show that there are no philosophical arguments which compel us to be dualists." Rather than mounting a positive defense of his view, the vast majority of the paper consists in rebutting objections to it.

There is, however, one passage where Smart summarizes his reasons for believing in physicalism. In explaining why he wants to resist the suggestion that we need to posit something "irreducibly psychical" in order to account for mental states – and here Smart is focused specifically on sensations – he says this:

> It seems to me that science is increasingly giving us a viewpoint whereby organisms are able to be seen as physicochemical mechanisms: it seems that even the behavior of man himself will one day be explicable in mechanistic terms. There does seem to be, so far as science is concerned, nothing in the world but increasingly complex arrangements of physical constituents. All except for one place: in consciousness. That is, for a full description of what is going on in a man you would have to mention not only the physical processes in his tissues, glands, nervous system, and so forth, but also his states of consciousness: his visual, auditory, and tactual sensations, his aches and pains. ... [S]ensations, states of consciousness, do seem to be the one sort of thing left outside the physicalist picture, and for various reasons I just cannot believe that this can be so. That everything should be explicable in terms of physics ... except the occurrence of sensations seems to me frankly unbelievable.

In fact, there seem to be two distinct considerations operating in this paragraph, one concerning simplicity, and one concerning the explanatory power of science. We will address each of them in what follows.

SIMPLICITY

When considerations of simplicity are invoked in the debate between dualism and physicalism – as well as in philosophy more generally – they tend to be referred to as **Ockham's Razor**. In the medieval period, philosopher William of Ockham suggested that "*pluralitas non est ponenda sine necessitate*," or, as it is usually stated, entities should not be posited beyond necessity. (A more literal translation would be: plurality should not be posited without necessity.) Ockham was by no means the first philosopher to introduce considerations of simplicity into the philosophical discussion. More than 1500 years prior, Aristotle had noted in his *Posterior Analytics* that "We may assume the superiority *ceteris paribus* of the demonstration which derives from fewer postulates or hypotheses – in short from fewer premises." But for whatever reason, this principle of simplicity has come to be associated with Ockham. As for why his principle is referred to as a razor, the thought seems to be that any unnecessary elements in one's theory should be shaved off.

That Ockham's Razor supports physicalism might initially seem to be obvious. After all, dualism posits two kinds of entities or properties where physicalism posits only one. Doesn't that mean that physicalism is the simpler theory and hence that it should be preferred? The matter cannot be resolved quite this quickly and easily, however, as the principle does not simply recommend that additional entities should never be postulated but that they should not be postulated *beyond necessity*. Dualists claim that physicalist explanations are inadequate and thus that the postulation of non-physical mentality is necessary. Both parties to the debate may well agree that when we have two different hypotheses that explain the phenomena equally well, we should go with the simpler hypothesis. The debate between dualism and physicalism need not be seen as a debate about the validity of Ockham's Razor. Rather, it can be seen as a debate about whether the two hypotheses really do explain the relevant phenomena – phenomena such as beliefs, pains, sensations, and so on – equally well.

In addition to this issue about explanatory capability, additional issues arise when we try to pin down precisely what is meant by simplicity, that is, in what sense of simplicity should a simpler theory be preferred. This matter has received more attention from metaphysicians and philosophers of science than from philosophers of mind. In those discussions, simplicity is generally treated as having two distinct interpretations. The first, often referred to as *elegance*, concerns the number of fundamental principles postulated by a theory. The second, often referred to as *parsimony*, concerns the number of kinds of entities postulated by a theory. Insofar as considerations of simplicity favor physicalism over dualism, this is on grounds of parsimony, not elegance. Attempts to defend the principle of parsimony, however, take us back to the issue of explanatory capability. What makes a more parsimonious theory preferable to a less parsimonious theory is its elimination of the kinds of entities that are explanatorily idle. But of course, whether mental kinds are explanatorily idle is precisely the point at issue in the debate between physicalists and dualists. Since physicalists tend to invoke considerations from science to defend their claim about the idleness of mentality, it looks as though this first general motivation for physicalism, considerations of simplicity, really boils down to the second general motivation for physicalism, considerations from the explanatory power of science.

THE EXPLANATORY POWER OF SCIENCE

There are at least two different dimensions to the physicalist's invocation of the explanatory power of science in defense of their view. The first concerns causal closure; the second concerns the past record of scientific success. We have already encountered the concerns relating to causal closure in our discussion of interactionist dualism in the previous chapter, but it will here be worth spelling out the argument so that it can more easily be seen as an argument for physicalism rather than as an objection to interactionism.

Physicalist David Papineau has recently laid out this reasoning in a particularly clear way:

Many effects that we attribute to conscious causes have full physical causes. But it would be absurd to suppose that these effects are caused twice over. So the conscious causes must be identical to some part of those physical causes.

(Papineau 2002)

To help demonstrate the force of the argument, he then gives a specific example. Suppose you walk to the fridge to get a drink because you are consciously feeling thirsty. In this kind of case, we are inclined to think it's your conscious thirst that causes you to walk to the fridge. But your walking is a bodily movement, and modern science suggests that your bodily movements are fully and completely caused by physical processes occurring in your brain and nervous system. Thus, says Papineau, "the obvious conclusion is that the conscious thirst must be identical with some part of those physical processes."

We can summarize in standard form as follows:

1   Conscious mental occurrences have physical effects E.
2   All physical effects are fully caused by purely physical events.
3   Therefore, physical effects E are fully caused by purely physical events. [From 2]
4   Physical effects E aren't always overdetermined by two distinct causes.
5   If physical effects E have conscious mental occurrences as causes and have purely physical events as causes, and there is no overdetermination, then the conscious mental occurrences and the purely physical events must be the *same cause*, that is, conscious mental occurrences must be identical to purely physical events.
6   Therefore, conscious mental occurrences must be identical to purely physical events. [From 1, 3,4,5]
7   Therefore, physicalism is true. [From 6]

The plausibility of this argument obviously depends in large part on the plausibility of premise 2, the causal closure principle. What evidence do we have for its truth? Often the evidence is thought to come from laws of conservation of matter and energy. Importantly, causal closure is not entailed directly by these laws. Insofar as conservation laws are defined in terms of a set of basic, fundamental forces, we need a further argument to establish that all such forces are physical. In offering such an argument, the physicalist might advert to the fact that, in the history of scientific inquiry, scientists have never discovered any forces other than physical forces at work. Moreover, when any new forces seem to be discovered, they have been shown to be reducible to the same group of fundamental forces as previously known forces. Thus, even though we may seem to come across forces that seem to us to be mental, the history of science suggests that these forces too will be reducible to the same fundamental forces – forces that are wholly physical – as all other known forces.

In addition to these considerations from causal closure, physicalism also gains plausibility just from general considerations about the progress of science and scientific explanation. Think of how many apparent mysteries have been dispelled by scientific progress – from how diseases spread to how genetic information is encoded, and so on. For our purposes, what's most important is how much we now know about the brain. When you compare the state of such knowledge in the early 1800s, or even the early 1900s, with the state of such knowledge in the early 2000s, the amount of progress made is simply staggering. Moreover, given the development in the 1970s of neural imagining techniques, the pace of this progress has quickened. As scientists learn more and more about the brain, aspects about human cognitive capabilities that previously seemed completely mysterious now seem considerably less so. Thus, insofar as dualism gains support from the sense that science can't possibly explain everything, that the mind is far too mysterious to be captured by mere science, the success of science with respect to solving other mysteries lends support to physicalism.

DIFFERENT VERSIONS OF PHYSICALISM

Now that we have seen some of the general motivations for a physicalist view, it is time to look more specifically at different versions of physicalism. We will here focus primarily on two such versions: the **identity theory** and **eliminative materialism**. While the identity theory is a reductive theory, one that aims to reduce mental states to physical states, eliminative materialism aims to do away with mental states altogether.

THE IDENTITY THEORY

The identity theory came to prominence in the 1950s via the work of three different philosophers: U.T. Place, Herbert Feigl, and J.J.C. Smart (whose work we mentioned briefly above). As we have seen, an interactionist dualist like Descartes takes the mind and brain to stand in a relationship of two-way causal interaction. In contrast, identity theorists like Place, Feigl, and Smart take the mind and brain to stand in a relationship of identity. In their view, mental states are not caused by brain states, but are identical to them.

Importantly, there are two different ways to identify mental states with brain states. One might draw the identity at the level of types, resulting in a theory known as **type physicalism**, or one might draw the identity at the level of tokens, resulting in a theory known as **token physicalism**. To understand the distinction between types and tokens, consider the television show *Wheel of Fortune*. Contestants trying to solve a word puzzle often spend $250 to buy a vowel. The purchase of the vowel E, for example, costs the contestant $250 no matter how many Es there are – whether the puzzle is *beekeeper* or *honeycomb*. In other words, the contestant buys a letter *type,* and Vanna White then reveals every *token* of the letter type that was purchased. Outside of *Wheel of Fortune*, purchases typically don't work this way. When you go to a car dealership and the dealer tells you (perhaps after considerable haggling) that the Prius costs $23,000, your check for that amount entitles you only to one token car and not to all the tokens of the Prius type on the lot.

As this discussion suggests, sometimes we talk of objects at the level of types and sometimes at the level of tokens. Likewise, when claiming that mental states are identical to brain states, we might be talking about mental state types or we might be talking about mental state tokens. Type identity claims are stronger than – and indeed entail – token identity claims. Given that water is H_2O, i.e., that the type *water* is identical to the type H_2O, it follows that every token water droplet is identical to a token H_2O droplet. But token identity claims do not entail type identity claims. Consider the mug that I have on my desk. On one side it has the Amherst College seal, on the other side it says Class of 1990, and it is made of ceramic. But while this token mug is identical to a ceramic object of such and such shape, it is not true that the type *mug* is identical to the type *ceramic object of such and such shape*. After all, some mugs are glass objects, some are wooden objects, and so on. Though the identity theorists of the 1950s did not explicitly draw the type/token distinction, the identity theory should be seen as a theory at the level of types and is seen as a version of type physicalism.

Consider a sample identification often used in philosophical discussion of the identity theory: pain is identical to c-fiber firing. Granted, as philosophers of mind well recognize, this claim is almost certainly false. Although there are indeed c-fibers in the brain, and although they appear to be in some way involved in the experience of pain, it's unlikely that c-fiber firing is quite the right brain state to identify with pain. Once we figure out exactly what the right brain state is, we can refine this identity claim, but in the meantime, this claim is used as a placeholder for the kind of psychophysical identity that the identity theorist wants to posit.

The identity theorists themselves are not involved in the enterprise of determining what the right brain state is. That determination is a matter for science. In this way, the identity theorists see psychophysical identities as analogous to other scientific discoveries, such as the discovery that water is H_2O, the discovery that temperature is mean molecular kinetic energy, or the discovery that lightning is electrical discharge.

In drawing an analogy to scientifically discovered identities, the identity theorists emphasize several related features of such identities. Some of these features are epistemic, i.e., they deal with how these identities come to be known. For example, the identity theorists stress that the plausibility of their theory hinges on the recognition that not all identities come to be known in the same way. Many identities – like the claims that "red is a color" and "a square is an equilateral rectangle" – can be known **a priori**, i.e., our knowledge of them does not depend on experience but rather depends only on our grasping the concepts involved in the claim. In contrast, an identity like "lightning is electrical discharge" can be known only **a posteriori**; it is an empirical claim that results from scientific inquiry. The identity theorist wants to understand psychophysical identities on the model of claims like "lightning is

electrical discharge" rather than claims like "a square is an equilateral rectangle." Claims like "pain is c-fiber firing" are also the
result of scientific inquiry and thus cannot be known a priori.

In addition to making these epistemic points, the identity theorists also draw attention to several important semantic features of
the psychophysical identities. Early in the 20th century, work by
German philosopher Gottlob Frege in philosophy of language had
shown that two expressions that refer to the same object may
nonetheless differ in meaning by having different senses. Looking
up into the nighttime sky, the ancient Greeks saw a heavenly body
that they called *the Evening Star*. Looking up into the morning sky,
they also saw a heavenly body that they called *the Morning Star*.
Unbeknownst to them, both of these heavenly bodies were really
the planet Venus. This gives us a case where two expressions,
"the Morning Star" and "the Evening Star," refer to the same
object while having different senses – the sense of the former
expression is something like "the last heavenly body visible in the
morning sky," while the sense of the latter expression is something like "the first heavenly body visible in the evening sky."
This distinction between sense and reference comes into play
whenever we have scientifically discovered identities. Though the
word "lightning" refers to the same phenomenon as the words
"electrical discharge," these two expressions do not have the same
sense. Likewise, though the word "pain" refers to the same phenomenon as the words "c-fiber firing," these two expressions do
not have the same sense.

These epistemic and semantic points are important for the
identity theorists because they help to block various objections that
might otherwise arise. We might worry, for example, that the
identification of pain with c-fiber firing is implausible, because
people can know that they are in pain without knowing that
they are in a state of c-fiber firing, and people can talk about
their pains without talking about c-fiber firings. After all, lots of
people have never even heard of c-fibers! By emphasizing that
pain can be identical to c-fiber firing even though the expressions "pain" and "c-fiber firing" have different meanings, and
even though we might well understand both terms without
knowing that they pick out the same thing, these worries can
be laid to rest.

PROBLEMS FOR THE IDENTITY THEORY

Since type identity claims entail token identity claims, type physicalism entails that every token pain is identical to a token c-fiber firing. This leads to one influential objection to the identity theory that cannot be laid to rest as easily as the worries we just explored. Consider an octopus. Research has shown that the pain-related behavior of an octopus is very similar to the pain-related behavior manifested by vertebrates. To give just a few examples, octopuses groom and protect injured body parts, they withdraw from harmful stimuli, and when they are touched near an injury they are more likely to swim away and squirt ink than when they are touched near a part of their body that is not injured. So it seems reasonable to assume that an octopus feels pain. But the octopus brain is dramatically different from a human brain. In fact, an octopus's neurons aren't even confined to its head but are also located in its arms. Given the vast differences between the octopus brain and the human brain, it is unlikely that the brain state that occurs when an octopus experiences pain is the same kind of brain state that occurs when we feel pain – whether that human brain state is c-fiber firing or something else. But if we have some instances of pain that are c-fiber firing and some instances that are not, then type physicalism is false.

Perhaps these considerations don't initially seem very worrying. Since octopuses are so different from humans, it might seem plausible to deny that octopuses feel the same kind of sensation when they are in pain than humans feel when we are in pain, and we might thus conclude that octopus pain is a different mental type from human pain. If octopus pain and human pain are different mental types, then they can each be identified with different brain state types – just as (human) pain and itches are identified with different brain state types.

But now consider a different example. Although the technology is not yet available, surgeons might one day be able to replace damaged parts of the human brain with mechanical substitutes in much the same way that they can now replace faulty heart valves with mechanical ones. Suppose that someone is involved in a car accident and suffers a severe injury to some of their c-fibers. After extensive surgery, doctors are able to remove the damaged c-fibers and replace them with a synthetic substitute. If the patient claims that she experiences no difference in her pain sensations before and after surgery – the pain she feels now when she steps on a stray Lego piece is just like the pain she felt previously when she stepped on a stray Lego piece – then we would have a case where we have some instances of human pain that are c-fiber firings and some instances that are not. So again, type physicalism would be false.

The objection we have here been exploring is often referred to as the **multiple realizability** objection, since the considerations we have just discussed suggest that pain can be realized in a multitude of different physical states. Worries about multiple realizability have played a big role in the rise of **functionalism**, the theory we will consider in Chapter Four.

Given this problem for type physicalism, one might wonder whether the identity theorist would do better to retreat to token physicalism. Even if it is not true that mental state types can be identified with physical state types, perhaps it's nonetheless true that every mental state is identical to some physical state. While some token pains might be identical with c-fiber firings, and some with an octopus-neuron-state, and some with a synthetic/mechanical state, they would all be tokens of some physical state or other.

In making this retreat, however, the identity theory would in many ways be giving up on the very task that they were aiming to accomplish. One large component of what we are looking for when we are looking for a theory of mind is an explanation of mentality, an explanation of what makes a mental state mental. A type physicalist theory gives us an answer to this question: a mental state is mental by virtue of being a brain state. Perhaps this answer is not entirely satisfying, as there are various brain states that we don't consider to be mental states. Consider, for example, the brain states involved in unconscious processes such as the control and regulation of breathing. But we do get some kind of unifying explanation, and we can also see the potential for a more complete and satisfying answer as the type physicalist further refines their theory. The token physicalist, however, really doesn't have any answer to this question. For them, all that can be said about what makes a mental state mental is that it is a physical state. And given the vast and varied examples of physical states that are not mental – from the states of rocks and radiators to the states of dandelions and dictionaries – we haven't been provided with any explanation of mentality. Worse, it's hard to see how the theory even has the potential for an answer.

The identity theory is a reductive theory of mind. It aims to reduce mental states to physical states of the brain. Dualists view this reductive project as hopeless because they think of the mental as existing over and above the physical. Some physicalist philosophers also view this reductive project as hopeless but for reasons quite different from those of the dualist. Rather than thinking of mental states as something in need of explanation, they think of mental states as something to be eliminated from our philosophical theorizing. In pursuing this line, such philosophers develop a physicalist theory known as **eliminative materialism**. The philosophers most closely associated with eliminative materialism are Paul and Patricia Churchland, a married couple who have made important contributions to this debate both jointly and individually.

Eliminative materialism starts from the fact that much of our intuitive understanding of the world has proven to be mistaken, even radically so. The theoretical beliefs of ordinary folks – belief sets we might think of as folk physics, folk biology, and so on – are often in conflict with the theories that have been developed by researchers trained in physics and biology and so on. Plato famously believed that the stars and planets were embedded in a heavenly sphere that rotated daily, and this belief persisted among the general public until the Scientific Revolution. Aristotle famously believed that heavier objects fall more quickly than lighter objects, and even today, many people intuitively cling to this false belief. These are just two examples among many of intuitive beliefs that have been shown to be false by subsequent scientific developments.

But why should we think that our intuitive understanding of mind fares any better? Eliminative materialism suggests that our ordinary understanding of mind should also be seen as a folk theory, a theory that we use to predict and explain the behavior of others. For example, when you try to figure out why your partner didn't text you back last night, you're likely to come up with an explanation in terms of various mental states. You might hypothesize that they were tired and didn't believe that you'd care if they waited until morning to respond, or you might instead hypothesize that they were still mad about a remark you'd made at lunch time and thus didn't want to interact with you. Maybe one of these particular explanations will turn out to be correct in this case, or maybe it won't, but as a general matter, folk theories are not very reliable. Given that folk physics and folk biology are infested with various misunderstandings, the eliminative materialists suggest that our folk psychology is likely problematic in the same way. And just as we have abandoned various aspects of folk physics and folk biology when they proved not to be explanatorily useful – aspects that the eliminative materialists refer to as *theoretical posits* – so too should we be prepared to abandon various aspects of folk psychology – in this case, theoretical posits like belief, desire, intention, emotion, and so on – in cases where they do not turn out to be explanatorily useful. In such cases, rather than trying to reduce mental states to physical states, we should instead just eliminate such mental notions entirely.

This reasoning, which we'll call the *Argument from the Falsity of Folk Psychology,* can be cast in standard form as follows:

1   Mental states like beliefs and desires are theoretical posits of folk psychology.
2   Folk psychology is false.
3   The theoretical posits of false theories do not exist.
4   Therefore, beliefs and desires do not exist. [From 1,2,3]

In defense of premise 3, the eliminative materialists often invoke examples from the past where we have subsequently discarded elements that had been posited by the theory in the past. In the 17th century, alchemists like J.J. Becher postulated the existence of a fire-like element called *phlogiston* to explain combustion. Proponents of the phlogiston theory believed that some substances, those that burn in air, contained phlogiston. When such substances burn, the phlogiston is released into the air. Phlogiston theory was dominant until the late 18th century when research by Antoine-Laurent Lavoisier showed that combustion was a chemical reaction involving oxygen. Though phlogiston theorists initially tried to adjust their theories to accommodate

Lavoisier's research, it eventually became clear that the phlogiston theory was doomed. Importantly, these scientific advances did not show that phlogiston was really a fuel, or that it was really an oxidant; rather, they showed that there was no such thing as phlogiston. Phlogiston was thus eliminated from chemical theory.

But why should we think that folk psychology is false? The Churchlands offer several different sorts of considerations. First, as we saw above, folk theories tend to have bad track records. Second, folk psychology is stagnant, i.e., it hasn't made any progress in several thousand years. We are still operating with the same basic folk psychological notions as ancient philosophers such as Plato and Aristotle, and we are only marginally better able than they were to explain behavior in terms of such notions. Third, there are lots of questions about mental phenomena that folk psychology does not seem to have the resources to answer: what is mental illness? What is the psychological function of sleep? How do we construct a three-dimensional visual image from the two-dimensional stimulations in our retina? What accounts for our ability to retrieve information from memory at such a blazingly fast speed? Having given examples of this sort, Paul Churchland notes that these are just some of the many mental phenomena about which folk psychology "sheds negligible light."

PROBLEMS FOR ELIMINATIVE MATERIALISM

Despite these limitations of folk psychology, however, opponents of eliminative materialism have often suggested that folk psychology is not in nearly as bad shape as the Churchlands suggest. After all, in ordinary life, we do enjoy a reasonably good track record at predicting the behavior of others. Such success might very well be taken to suggest that folk psychology is at least roughly true. Though it might be in need of refinement, its usefulness argues against its wholesale rejection.

One also might worry that, given our current understanding of the brain, it is far too early to take a stance on the truth of eliminative materialism. At this stage, eliminative materialism might really be seen simply as making a prediction rather than offering a theory. The eliminative materialists predict that, once we have a more developed understanding of neuroscience, it is unlikely that the posits of folk psychology will be retained. But perhaps the development of neuroscience will go differently from what they now expect. And even if they're right, that's not to say that *all* of the mental states posited by folk psychology will be discarded. After all, there are plenty of posits of folk physics that have survived the development of physics. So perhaps there are at least some mental states that will survive the development of neuroscience.

Finally, many philosophers have worried that eliminative materialism is a self-refuting theory. This objection, often referred to as the self-refutation objection, starts from the thought that the eliminative materialists themselves are making various assertions, and the making of an assertion seems to require the existence of beliefs. For the eliminative materialists to assert their theory, they must believe it, but that suggests that there really are beliefs, and thus eliminative materialism shows itself to be false. Put very roughly, we might see this objection as making the following claim: the eliminative materialists seem to be committed to saying something like, "I believe that there are no beliefs," and that claim itself seems incoherent. In response, the eliminative materialists typically deny that making assertions commits them to positing the existence of beliefs. To assume such a commitment, they would argue, would be to beg the question against their theory.

GENERAL PROBLEMS FOR PHYSICALISM

Given the dialectic between dualism and physicalism, many of the arguments for dualism can be seen as arguments against physicalism. The Conceivability Argument and the Zombie Argument, as well as the other arguments considered in Chapter Two, fall into this category. In this section, we will consider additional problems for physicalism over and above the arguments that we have considered in support of dualism. Though earlier in this chapter we looked at problems arising for particular versions of physicalism, the two problems we will now consider are meant to apply to physicalist views of all stripes.

The first arises from considerations having to do with phenomenological features of experience, or **qualia**. Physicalist views have long been accused of failing to account adequately for the qualitative aspects of our mental life. Our exploration of this problem will center primarily on one particular argument that has been especially influential in recent decades, namely, *the Knowledge Argument*, though we will first consider a related argument known as *the Bat Argument* that has also been highly influential.

The second problem arises from considerations having to do with the coherence of the physicalist position. Our exploration of this problem will center on an issue known as *Hempel's dilemma*.

THE BAT ARGUMENT

Is there something it's like to be a rock? Here it seems plausible that the answer is a resounding no. But is there something that it's like to be a bat? Here most people are inclined to answer in the affirmative. After all, bats are mammals. Just as we attribute qualitative experience to mammals such as humans, gorillas, and dogs, it seems plausible that bats too have qualitative experience.

What it's like to be a gorilla or a dog probably differs in various ways from one another, and also from what it's like to be a human, but it's also likely that the qualitative experience of all three of these creatures has much in common with one another. When it comes to the bat, however, their qualitative experience seems likely to be radically different from the qualitative experience of humans. Unlike humans, gorillas, and dogs, bats navigate the world by echolocation and are able to use sound to "see" objects in their environment.

In his famous paper "What Is It Like To Be a Bat?" Thomas Nagel (1974) takes the fact that bat experience is radically different from our own to support the conclusion that we cannot know what it is like to a bat – not only can we not experience anything like it, but we can't even imagine anything like it. This in turn leads him to be skeptical about the prospects of physicalism. In short, he takes his reflections on bat experience to show that what it is like to be a bat is fundamentally a subjective phenomenon, one that cannot be captured from another point of view such as a human's. But since physicalism takes the objective point of view, then physicalism cannot capture what it's like to be a bat. The physicalist story leaves out something essential about the nature of experience.

Nagel himself stops short of inferring the falsity of physicalism from the argument that he sets forth. Rather, he concludes only that we currently lack the conceptual resources to see how physicalism could be true. Many other philosophers of mind go further than Nagel, however, and assume that if the argument is successful then physicalism must be false.

ASSESSING THE BAT ARGUMENT

Though one could unravel the bat argument by denying that bats have qualitative experience, physicalists have generally not pursued this line of response. A potentially more plausible strategy is to take issue with Nagel's claim that bat phenomenology is so vastly different from human phenomenology. There are two ways this strategy might be developed.

First, we might draw on considerations from neuroscience to suggest that some of Nagel's underlying assumptions are implausible. For example, Nagel seems to assume that there are systematic correlations between physiology and phenomenology. It's because bat physiology is so different from human physiology that Nagel assumes that the phenomenology must also be so different. But it's not clear that physiology and phenomenology are correlated in exactly the way that Nagel thinks.

Second, we might draw directly on phenomenological considerations. Some blind people use something akin to echolocation to help them navigate their surroundings. Assuming suitable attention and practice, perhaps sighted people could employ such techniques as well. Additionally, given developments in virtual reality technology, perhaps we can have a virtual echolocatory experience. Even if these experiences are not exactly like a bat's experience, they may give us enough material to get our imaginations going, and we might thereby be able to come to know what a bat's experience is like. If this is right, then Nagel would be wrong to think that bat experience is inaccessible from a different point of view.

THE KNOWLEDGE ARGUMENT

The Knowledge Argument against physicalism, proposed by Frank Jackson in his article "Epiphenomenal Qualia," (1982) centers on a thought experiment that is often referred to as *the Mary case*. As Jackson describes her, Mary is a brilliant scientist who lives at some point in the future when color science has been completed and we have achieved a complete understanding of what color is and how color vision works. There are two very important facts about Mary. First, though Mary has fully functional color vision, she has spent her entire life trapped in a black and white room and has never had a color sensation. There are various other details that would need to be filled in to make this work. The room couldn't have any mirrors or reflective surfaces, for example, and she'd have to be wearing gloves of some sort, and so on. But suppose that these details are all filled in appropriately. Second, Mary has mastered the entirety of the completed color science. From reading lots of textbooks, and from watching various videos and lectures electronically (all in black and white, of course), Mary has learned everything that science has to teach us about color and color vision. As Jackson puts it, she has learned all of the physical facts about color.

Now here's the interesting part: one day Mary is released from her black and white room and finally has her first color sensation. Suppose, for example, that she is shown a ripe tomato. When she has her first sensation of red, what happens? In particular, does she learn something new?

In putting forth this case, Jackson has the strong intuition that she does learn something new. It seems pretty natural that when Mary sees the tomato for the first time, she'll have what we might call an "Aha!" reaction, as in "Aha! So that's what seeing red is like." But if Mary learns something new, then given that she already knew all of the physical facts about color while she was in the room, it must be that those physical facts don't tell the whole story about color. From this, Jackson draws the conclusion that physicalism must be false.

We can summarize the Knowledge Argument in standard form as follows:

1   While in the room, Mary has acquired all the physical facts there are about color sensations, including the sensation of seeing red.

2   When Mary exits the room and sees a ripe red tomato, she learns a new fact about the sensation of seeing red, namely its subjective character.

3   Therefore, there are non-physical facts about color sensations. [From 1,2]
4   If there are non-physical facts about color sensations, then color sensations are non-physical events.
5   Therefore, color sensations are non-physical events. [From 3,4]
6   If color sensations are non-physical events, then physicalism is false.
7   Therefore, physicalism is false. [From 5,6]

ASSESSING THE KNOWLEDGE ARGUMENT

Most philosophers who imagine the Mary case agree that she'll have an "Aha!" reaction when she sees the ripe tomato for the first time. Perhaps the two most prominent dissenters on this front are Daniel Dennett (1991) and Paul Churchland (1985, 1989), both of whom claim that our intuitions about the case cannot be trusted. Dennett, for example, claims that the only reason we think Mary will have the "Aha!" reaction is that we are not really imagining what we are supposed to imagine when we are presented with the Mary case. Rather than imagine that Mary knows *all* the physical facts inside the room, which is hard to imagine, we instead simply imagine that she knows *lots and lots* of these facts, something much easier to imagine. If we really imagined that Mary knew the complete physical story about color, we would no longer conclude that she is at all surprised when she leaves the room.

Dennett and Churchland aside, even most physicalists share Jackson's sense that Mary will have an "Aha!" reaction when she leaves the room, and so much of the discussion about the knowledge argument has centered on whether her "Aha" reaction justifies premise 2, that is, whether her "Aha!" reaction shows that she has learned a new fact. There are three different strategies that have been pursued in this vein: the ability analysis, the acquaintance analysis, and the old fact/new guise analysis.

Of these three strategies, the ability analysis is probably the most popular. Proponents of this analysis start by reminding us of the distinction between factual knowledge and ability knowledge, or what is often called *knowledge-that* and *knowledge-how*. Suppose you're trying to get your driver's license in California. Part of what's required is a written examination in which you have to demonstrate your knowledge of lots of facts about driving, for example, that when driving within 500 to 1000 feet of a school the speed limit is 25 mph unless otherwise posted, that a painted red curb means no stopping, standing, or parking, that when driving in fog you should use your low-beam headlights, and so on. But another part of what's required is an on-road driving test in which you have to demonstrate your driving ability, for example, the ability to maintain good control of your vehicle, to complete left- and right-hand turns, to back up your vehicle safely, and so on. While the written examination tests your knowledge-that, the on-road driving examination tests your knowledge-how.

In general, ability knowledge, knowledge-how, does not seem to reduce to factual knowledge, knowledge-that. Someone might know all the relevant facts relating to the safe operation of a car and yet lack the ability to drive. Someone might know all the relevant facts relating to juggling and yet lack the ability to juggle. When they finally acquire the ability to drive, or the ability to juggle, this does not consist in their learning any additional facts; rather, it consists in their gaining some know-how that they previously lacked.

Now consider Mary's knowledge of what a sensation is like, what we'll call *what it's like knowledge*, or *WIL knowledge*. Proponents of the ability analysis suggest that we should think of WIL knowledge not as factual knowledge but rather as ability knowledge. When Mary exits the room and sees a ripe tomato for the first time, she does learn something, but her learning does not consist in the acquisition of knowledge-that. Rather, it consists in the acquisition of knowledge-how. Once she sees the ripe tomato, she gains abilities that she'd previously lacked. David Lewis, one of the chief proponents of the ability analysis, claims that Mary gains the abilities to recognize, remember, and imagine the sensation of red (Lewis 1988). Knowing what the sensation of red is like consists in the possession of these abilities.

In this way, proponents of the ability analysis can grant that Mary has the "Aha!" reaction without granting that she learns a new fact about the sensation of red. They thus deny premise 2 of the argument above. The plausibility of this kind of response to the Knowledge Argument depends on whether we can adequately capture WIL knowledge in terms of abilities. Concerning the abilities that Lewis specifically mentions, some philosophers have worried about whether any of them is really necessary for WIL knowledge. Someone with a memory deficiency such that they are incapable of forming new memories may know what seeing red is like even though they can't remember what it's like. Likewise, someone with a very bad imagination may also know what seeing red is like even though they can't imagine what it's like.

Like the ability analysis, the acquaintance analysis disputes premise 2 of the Knowledge Argument. Also, like the ability analysis, the acquaintance analysis argues that Mary can learn something new without acquiring factual knowledge. But unlike proponents of the ability analysis, proponents of the acquaintance analysis are not focused on knowledge-how but acquaintance knowledge. Suppose you have never been to Sydney before. In anticipation of an upcoming vacation, you read all the guidebooks, look at maps, scour the web for information about it, and so on. If you work at it hard enough, you might come to know all the facts about Sydney there are to know. Still, it seems that you learn something new when you arrive in the city for the first time. Now that you are acquainted with it, you come to know it in a way that you didn't before. Proponents of the acquaintance analysis argue that something similar happens to Mary when she finally has a sensation of red. Though she doesn't come to learn any new facts, she learns something new simply in that she is now acquainted with it.

As with the ability analysis, the plausibility of this response depends on whether we can adequately capture WIL knowledge in terms of acquaintance. Moreover, here we might worry about whether becoming acquainted with someone or something really counts as learning something new. Would acquaintance with something that we know all the facts about really provoke the "Aha!" reaction?

In denying premise 2, proponents of both the ability analysis and the acquaintance analysis accept that Mary learns something new when she leaves the room. What's at issue for these analyses is whether she learns a new fact. Though the old fact/new guise analysis also denies premise 2, proponents of this analysis do not accept that Mary learns something new. Yes, she may have an "Aha!" reaction. But, say proponents of this analysis, that's simply because she comes to appreciate an old fact, a fact that she already knew, in a new way. When she has the sensation of red for the first time, she can now represent a fact she already knew under a new phenomenal guise.

A detailed discussion of this response would require us to delve into murky matters about how exactly facts should be individuated, but we can flesh out the basic idea without things getting too complicated. In general, there are many ways to capture the same worldly fact. The sentence *Bruce Wayne is 6'2" tall* and the sentence *Bruce Wayne is 1.8796 meters tall* both express the same fact, namely, that a certain man has a certain property. If you know that Bruce Wayne is identical to Batman, you can express this same fact about the man's height in another way: *Batman is 6'2" tall*. Moreover, if you know French, you could now express this same fact in yet another way: *Bruce Wayne est de 1.8796 mètres*. For proponents of the old fact/new guise analysis, what happens when Mary leaves the room is that she's now able to express an old fact in a new way. One way to spell this out is in terms of *phenomenal concepts*. By having the sensation of red, Mary comes to acquire a phenomenal concept of red. Whereas previously she could express the relevant fact as something like: *the sensation of red has brain property 796*, she can now express the relevant fact as something like: *the sensation of red feels like this*. As is probably clear, whether physicalists can successfully use the old fact/new guise analysis in responding to the Knowledge Argument depends on analyzing phenomenal concepts in such a way that they are compatible with their view.

WORRIES ABOUT THE COHERENCE OF THE NOTION OF QUALIA

Before concluding our discussion of the general problem for physicalism arising from phenomenological considerations, it is worth noting that some physicalists have suggested that these phenomenological considerations are inherently problematic. This line of argumentation is perhaps best associated with Daniel Dennett, who has argued that the notion of qualia is "so thoroughly confused" that we'd do best to abandon the notion altogether (1988).

In developing this argument, Dennett suggests that the traditional conception of qualia has four different aspects. Qualia are thought to be (1) ineffable, i.e., not describable in language; (2) intrinsic, i.e., a property a mental state has in and of itself and not in terms of its relation to anything else; (3) private; and (4) directly or immediately accessible in consciousness. He then offers a large variety of thought experiments – or what he calls intuition pumps – to show that nothing can actually meet these four criteria.

We can get a sense of his overall argument by considering a slightly amended version of one of these intuition pumps. Imagine two individuals Téa and Coco who have long worked as coffee tasters in the quality control division of a coffee company. Though they both agree that they no longer like the taste of their company's coffee, they disagree as to why. Téa says that her preferences have shifted over time. The coffee still tastes exactly the same to her, she reports, but she no longer likes that taste. Coco denies that her preferences have shifted, but she reports that the coffee doesn't taste the same to her anymore. To cast it as Dennett does, Téa explains her dislike of the coffee by postulating that her *tastes* have changed while Coco explains her dislike of the coffee by postulating her *tasters* have changed.

But now consider the following question: how does each know that she's right about what's happened to her? Perhaps Téa is really in the situation that Coco is in, or vice versa, or perhaps they are each in a situation that's midway between. If we accept that they could be mistaken, then it's not clear that qualitative experience is really directly or immediately apprehensible to consciousness. Insofar as we think they could not be mistaken, whatever story we tell is likely to draw on the fact that they no longer like the taste. But this seems to suggest a relational property of the coffee-tasting experience, and that means that the nature of the qualitative experience is not intrinsic to it. Thus, concludes Dennett, there is a deep incoherence in the very conception of qualia.

Although other philosophers have likewise worried about how exactly we can specify a coherent notion of qualia, it's fair to say that the wholesale rejection of qualia is a minority position. Among philosophers of mind today, the main controversy about qualia concerns their nature and not their existence.

HEMPEL'S DILEMMA

The worries about qualia we have been considering thus far call into question the adequacy of the physicalist theory. In contrast, the set of considerations we will now be turning to calls into question the coherence of the theory. The problem arises from considering the notion of the physical. In claiming that everything is physical, the physicalist owes us an explanation of what is meant by this notion. Typically, the explanation makes reference to physics. A property is physical if it falls into the domain of theories of physics. Granted, when the explanation is put this simply, obvious counterexamples immediately arise. *Being a rock* seems to be a paradigmatic physical property, but physical theories themselves don't tell us about this property. To get around these kinds of obvious counterexamples, we might say that a property is physical if it falls into the domain of physical theory or can be wholly explained by properties that fall into the domain of physical theory. While *having mass* is a property of the first sort, *being a rock* is a property of the second sort.

But now a further question arises: what physical theory does the physicalist have in mind? In answering this question, the physicalist faces a dilemma. Suppose they define physicalism in terms of our current physical theory. On this definition, physicalism will be almost certainly false, since our current physical theory is almost surely still incomplete. But suppose they have defined physicalism in terms of some future, ideal physics. On this definition, physicalism will be true, but it will also be trivial, since exactly what's covered by a future physics cannot be predicted, and it might even include properties that, on our current understanding at least, are the sorts of things that are purely mental.

To see more clearly the force of the second horn of the dilemma, it may help to consider the property *being a ghost*. Suppose that 22nd-century science finds strong evidence for the existence of immaterial ghosts, and they are unable to explain any of this evidence in terms of any already accepted physical properties such as having mass, having charge, and so on. As a result, they add the property *being made of ectoplasm* to their physical theory, and explain what it is to be a ghost in terms of it. Though intuitively the existence of ghosts should be incompatible with physicalism, once we define physicalism in terms of a future physics, we don't get this result. Physicalism thus becomes trivial. If anything that can't be explained in terms of accepted physical theory simply gets added as a new primitive element of that physical theory, then the notion of physical becomes an empty one.

As this problem was given a particularly forceful explication by the 20ᵗʰ-century German philosopher Carl Hempel, it is often referred to as **Hempel's dilemma**. While there are various responses that physicalists have made, the dilemma does seem to point to a problem in tying the notion of *physical* to the theory of physics. To save physicalism, then, one might look to alternate ways of getting a handle on the notion of the physical. For example, one option that has recently been explored by philosophers such as Barbara Montero (2001) attempts to shift our focus from the notion of the physical to the notion of the non-mental. The mind-body debate, on this construal, is not fundamentally about the physical vs. the non-physical but about the mental vs. the non-mental. Alternatively, the physicalist might respond by noting that Hempel's dilemma is as much a problem for the dualist as for the physicalist. If a viable notion of the physical is unavailable to us, then the dualist's claim that "the mind is not physical" would be just as problematic as the physicalist's claim that "the mind is physical."

CONCLUDING REMARKS

This chapter has introduced us to physicalism and the main considerations in support of it. These considerations – arising in part from methodological principles favoring simplicity and in part from the sense that our theory of mind should be scientifically respectable – are very powerful ones. In particular, the sense that dualism flies in the face of our scientific understanding of the world has led many philosophers to think that some version of physicalism must be the correct theory of mind.

Having reviewed the general case for physicalism, we looked more specifically at two different versions of physicalism: the identity theory and eliminative materialism. As we saw, each of these versions of physicalism has some proprietary advantages and some proprietary disadvantages. We then discussed some considerations that have been brought against physicalism in general – considerations stemming from the qualitative aspects of our mental life. Although the majority of contemporary philosophers embrace some version of physicalism, it remains to be seen whether physicalism can really account adequately for qualia. As we saw, a further problem facing physicalism arises from the way that the view is specified in reference to physics.

Given the issues that have been raised with both dualism and physicalism, one might naturally wonder whether there are other alternatives to consider. In recent years, a growing dissatisfaction with both dualism and physicalism has led a number of philosophers to look for some kind of different alternative or some kind of middle path between the two. The basic line of thought might be summed up roughly as follows: dualism respects what seems to be a basic fact about our existence as humans, namely that we have a robust mental life, that we are conscious. But in doing so, it seems to fly in the face of science. In contrast, physicalism accords nicely with our scientific understanding of the world. But in doing so, it seems unable to accommodate consciousness in any robust way. Isn't there some way that we can take science seriously while also taking consciousness seriously?

Recently, some philosophers have suggested that we can do so by reviving Russellian monism, a view associated with 20th-century British philosopher Bertrand Russell and that takes its inspiration from some of his remarks in *The Analysis of Matter*:

> Physics, in itself, is exceedingly abstract, and reveals only certain mathematical characteristics of the material with which it deals. It does not tell us anything as to the intrinsic character of this material.
>
> (Russell 1927/1954, 10)

Here Russell seems to be pointing to the fact that physics defines its basic entities only in structural or relational terms. But what underlies all of these structural and relational facts? It seems that there must be some underlying intrinsic or categorical properties to ground them. Perhaps these underlying properties, in addition to grounding the physical facts, could also give rise to consciousness. If so, then we would have a different kind of answer to the traditional mind-body problem.

Though proponents of Russellian monism claim that they can combine the best aspects of traditional dualism and traditional physicalism without inheriting the difficulties associated with those views, whether and to what extent the theory succeeds in these aims is still a matter of some dispute. Given that the theory of

Russellian monism has really only begun to receive serious scrutiny over the last fifteen to twenty years, it's probably too soon to be able to draw any definitive conclusions about the likelihood of its success.

There is, however, another alternative to dualism and physicalism that has received considerably more scrutiny over the past half century. According to functionalism, the mind shouldn't be defined in terms of the stuff it's made of but rather in terms of what it does, in terms of its function. We will consider this view in detail in Chapter Four.

FURTHER READING

Three classic papers associated with the development and defense of the identity theory are Smart (1959), Place (1956), and Feigl (1958). For development of eliminative materialism, see Paul Churchland (1981, 1988) and Patricia Churchland (1986).

For more about Ockham's Razor, see the entry on simplicity in the *Stanford Encyclopedia of Philosophy* (Baker 2016). For those readers looking for a book-length discussion on the topic, see Sober (2015). For more about the argument from causal closure, see Papineau (2002).

The original presentation of the Knowledge Argument appears in Jackson (1982); there is further discussion in Jackson (1986). Interestingly, Jackson has recently repudiated the Knowledge Argument (2007); he no longer believes that it successfully refutes physicalism.

For a discussion of an interesting real-life case that bears on the Knowledge Argument, see Sacks (1995). In this essay, Sacks describes the case of Virgil, a 50-year-old man who had been blind since childhood but whose sight is suddenly restored.

For two influential developments of the ability analysis, see Lewis (1988) and Nemirow (1990). For an influential development of the acquaintance analysis, see Conee (1985). A number of papers addressing the Knowledge Argument can be found in two recent anthologies: Alter and Walter (2007) and Ludlow, Nagasawa, and Stoljar (2005).

For discussion of Russellian monism, see Stoljar (2006) and Chalmers (1996), as well as the essays in Alter and Nagasawa (2015).

FUNCTIONALISM

Every year, hundreds and hundreds of raw eggs are dropped from the tops of multistorey buildings in school-sponsored Egg Drop Challenges. Prior to the drop, each egg is encased in an egg protection contraption built by a group of students. Some of the eggs survive the fall unscathed. Some do not. Successful egg protection contraptions – the ones that kept the egg from breaking – are constructed out of lots of different stuff. In one YouTube video featuring successful egg drops, the devices in use included a bubble-wrapped tissue box, a set of duct-taped balloons, and a bag of popcorn and flour.

Each of these descriptions captures the individual contraptions in physical terms. But if we tried to specify exactly what these contraptions have in common that makes them egg protectors, we wouldn't be able to do it in terms of specific physical materials. There are no particular physical materials that they all share. To capture what makes them egg protectors, we would have to talk about how the contraptions function. This basic distinction between physical specification and functional specification underlies the functionalist view of mind that we will discuss in this chapter. For the functionalists, to explain what the mind *is* we need to specify not what the mind is *made of* but rather what the mind *does*. We'll start with a discussion of the philosophical precedents that gave rise to the development of **functionalism**. We'll then turn to a closer look at the view itself – both what it is and whether it provides a plausible account of our mental lives.

THE ROOTS OF FUNCTIONALISM

BEHAVIORISM

Suppose you believe that there will be a major rainstorm later today. This belief is associated with all sorts of different behavior. You text your friend to cancel your plans for an outdoor picnic, you close your windows and turn off the automatic yard sprinklers, and you put on your rainboots and take an umbrella with you when you leave the house. In thinking about the relationship between your belief and this behavior, it's natural to think that belief *caused* the behavior. But according to a theory of mind popular in the early 20th century, this would be a mistake. Rather than seeing a causal relationship between mental states and behavior, the **behaviorists** identified mental states and behavior. What it is to have the belief that there will be a major rainstorm later today is not to be in some ghostly internal state but to be disposed to engage in a set of characteristic behaviors like the ones we just described. Likewise, what it is to have a pain in your left ankle is to be disposed to engage in a different set of characteristic behaviors – saying "ouch," rubbing the affected spot, wearing an ACE bandage, limping, and so on. Importantly, someone might be disposed to behave in a certain way without actually behaving that way. Behavioral dispositions are best understood as tendencies toward actions rather than actions themselves.

Like the **identity theory** and **eliminative materialism**, behaviorism is a **physicalist** theory. But unlike these other versions of physicalism, behaviorism has not really survived into the 21st century. Indeed, it had more or less died out by the 1960s. Although there probably still remain a handful of philosophers of mind with behaviorist leanings, there is a pretty widespread consensus that behaviorism is not a viable theory. The problem is not just its conflict with our pretheoretical intuitions about the relationship between mind and behavior. Given the difficulty of the mind-body problem, it's quite likely that the correct theory will be counterintuitive in at least some respects. Rather, what dooms behaviorism is the apparently obvious counterexamples to it. Not only are there cases in which someone is in a given mental state without any disposition whatsoever to behave in those characteristic ways, but there are also cases in which someone is disposed to behave in the ways characteristic of a given mental state without actually being in that state.

Consider someone who is extremely stoical, someone committed to concealing how they really feel. Let's call him Mort. And let's suppose that Mort's commitment runs really deep. After years of training, he is able to remain completely stone-faced in situations that are generally considered to be emotionally difficult or painful. When he steps on a sharp tack, or stubs his toe, he does not cry out or grimace, his eyes do not well up, and he does not engage in any characteristic pain-related behavior. Moreover, Mort's stoicism has become so ingrained that he even lacks any disposition to behave in any of these ways. His impassive reaction is completely natural to him. But despite his lack of any pain-related behavioral dispositions, it seems plausible that he's in a state of pain. After all, he just stepped on a tack! If this is a coherent scenario – that is, if there could be a stoic like Mort who's in pain despite lacking any of the relevant behavioral dispositions – then behaviorism must be false.

Next consider someone who is an extremely good stage performer, someone who excels at portraying a large variety of human feelings. Let's call her Mimi. After years of training, Mimi is able to behave exactly as someone does when they are in a painful situation even when she herself is not in that situation. Even when she hasn't stepped on a sharp tack, or stubbed her toe, or encountered any painful stimulus at all, she will sometimes cry out and grimace, with her eyes welling up, and with all the other behavior that is characteristic of having a pain in her foot. Moreover, she is able to do so entirely convincingly. No one around her can tell that it's all an elaborate performance. But despite all of this pain-related behavior, it seems plausible that she's not in a state of pain. After all, there's been no painful stimulus whatsoever! If the case of Mimi presents a coherent scenario – that is, if there could be a performer like Mimi who's not in pain despite evidencing all of the relevant pain behavior – then once again behaviorism must be false.

MORALS FROM BEHAVIORISM AND THE IDENTITY THEORY

Functionalists draw an important moral from these problems with behaviorism: an adequate theory of mind must be able to account for mentality even when there is not the appropriate behavior. But that's not to say that mental states have nothing to do with behavior whatsoever. As we will see, the functionalists agree with the behaviorists that behavior should play an important role in our analysis of mental states.

Functionalists also draw an important moral from one of the problems that plagued the **identity theory**. As we saw in the last chapter, the fact that mental states seem to be **multiply realizable** raises a problem for the identity theory. To remind us of the basic issue, let's use the example of the Heptapods, the enigmatic alien species from the movie *Arrival*. With their grey fleshy skin, their seven limbs, and their apparent lack of sensory apparatuses like eyes or mouths, the Heptapods clearly have a vastly different anatomy from humans. Their brains are surely made of far different stuff from neurons. But the Heptapods are highly intelligent, more so than humans, and they have a sophisticated system of communication. Once the human scientists are able to figure out how Heptapod language works, it becomes clear that the Heptapods make plans and have goals, and more generally, that they have conscious experiences. Consider one of those human scientists, Dr. Louise Banks (played by Amy Adams), and one of the Heptapods, the one the humans nickname Costello. At various points in the movie, it seems plausible that Dr. Banks and Costello both want to communicate, i.e., that they are in the very same kind of mental state as one another.

While this example is drawn from science fiction, the coherence of this kind of case suggests that mental states can be realized in vastly different physical structures – that they are multiply realizable. One doesn't need c-fibers, for example, to be in pain. But multiple realizability is incompatible with the identity theory. On that theory, Dr. Banks's mental states are identical with neural states. Given that Costello does not have any neurons and hence is never in any neural states, the identity theory would entail that Dr. Banks and Costello can never be in a mental state of the same type.

Functionalists draw an important moral from this shortcoming of the identity theory: an adequate theory of mind must be able to account for mental states exactly like ours even when there are not physical states exactly like ours. That's not to say that mental states have nothing whatsoever to do with brain states. But as we will see, the functionalists do not think that it's the physical make-up of the brain states that matter for mentality. Rather, what's important is what the brain states *do*, i.e., how they function.

Ultimately, functionalism can be seen as a direct outgrowth of behaviorism and the identity theory – an attempt to build on their insights and learn from their mistakes. Though the functionalists see brain and behavior as both important for mentality, they deny that mentality can be reduced either to behavior or to brain states. Unlike the eliminativist, however, the functionalist does not think that these reductive failures suggest that mental states need to be discarded. Rather, on the functionalist view, we can achieve a perfectly adequate understanding of mental states if we look at them in functional terms.

WHAT IS FUNCTIONALISM?

To understand what it means to specify something in functional rather than physical terms, it will be helpful to remind ourselves of two old sayings. First, it's often said that all that glitters is not gold. What it is for something to be a nugget of gold, for example, is not just for it to be a glittery thing but also for it to be composed of atoms with atomic number 79. Compare pyrite, or fool's gold, which has a similarly brilliant yellow luster but is a compound of iron sulfide. To count as gold, an item has to have a very specific physical constitution.

But now consider the second old saying: if you build a better mousetrap, the world will beat a path to your door. How do you build a better mousetrap? Do you need some particular physical stuff? The answer here is clearly no, at least according to lots and lots of do-it-yourself websites. To build the popular bucket mousetrap – and as at least one of these DIY websites declares, "there is *no* better mousetrap than this!" – it takes only a bucket, a dowel, a cylindrical object, a ramp, and some sticky bait. It doesn't matter what the bucket is made of, or what the dowel is made of, or what kind of food the bait is. All that matters is the functional set up – that the pieces are put together so that the mouse will climb up the ramp, jump onto the cylinder where the bait is placed, and then fall into the bucket by the spinning of the dowel that runs through the cylinder. (Fear not, mouse lovers, as the mouse doesn't fall far enough to be injured and so can easily be released back into the wild.)

According to functionalism, mental states are best understood on the model of mousetraps and not on the model of gold. To be a state like pain, what matters is function and not constitution.

FUNCTIONALIST SPECIFICATIONS OF MENTAL STATES

In setting out their vision for how mental states are to be analyzed, the functionalists often draw analogies to the functioning of machines. As a general matter, what a machine does depends on what internal state it is in when it receives a given input. The same input will not always result in the same output. Mental states work in an analogous way.

Consider the coin press machines often found at tourist sites. At Disneyland, for example, there are more than 150 different commemorative images that can be pressed onto pennies, nickels, dimes, and quarters. A pressed penny typically costs fifty cents plus the penny to be pressed, while a pressed quarter is usually seventy-five cents plus the quarter to be pressed. To make things simpler, however, let's consider the machines at the Eiffel Tower. There are three different machines, each with a specialized commemorative image, and at each machine, one pays two Euros to receive a pressed Euro. The machines accept only one and two Euro coins. What happens when you insert a one Euro coin? If this is the first coin to be inserted, then the machine won't do anything. It simply waits for you to insert a second Euro. If this is the second Euro to be inserted, then the machine will press a Euro and dispense it to you. What happens if you insert a two Euro coin? If this is the first coin to be inserted, the machine presses a Euro and dispenses it to you. But if you've previously inserted a one Euro coin, then the machine will press a Euro, dispense it to you, and also dispense a Euro in change.

This can all be expressed in the following chart, often referred to as a *machine table*. In reviewing this chart, it may help to metaphorically think of S1 as the state of *waiting for a one Euro coin* and S2 as the state of *waiting for a two Euro coin*.

Table 4.1 Machine table specification of a coin press machine

	One Euro coin input	*Two Euro coin input*
S1	Dispenses a pressed Euro; moves to S2	Dispenses a pressed Euro; dispenses a one Euro coin in change; moves to S2
S2	Moves to S1	Dispenses a pressed Euro; remains in S2

This same point applies to the functionalist analysis of mental states, an analysis that consists of three components: inputs, outputs, and relations to other states. Consider once again the case where you experience pain in your big toe. You enter this mental state as a result of some input: stepping on a tack, or coming into contact with the wall, or being in the path of a falling brick. This mental state also results in various outputs: grimacing, crying out, eyes welling up, and so on. Thus far, the analysis sounds just like a behaviorist analysis. But it's the third aspect of the functionalist analysis – the relations to other mental states – that differentiates the functionalist from the **behaviorist**. In some cases when you have pain in your toe you don't grimace or call out. This can be explained in terms of the mental state you were in when the painful inputs occurred. Did you then have the belief that you were in the campus library, where silence is expected? Or did you then have the desire not to call attention to yourself and your clumsiness? Either of these mental states will affect what output your pain induces. Moreover, your coming to be in pain might also lead to additional mental states: anger, embarrassment, or perhaps a newfound hatred for tacks. Setting all of this out in a chart would result in something much more complicated than the one we gave for the coin press machine, but then again, given the difference in complexity between the operation of a coin press machine and the operation of the human mind, this shouldn't be at all surprising.

For behaviorism, your disposition to behave in a certain way given certain inputs *is* your mental state. Like the identity theory, it is a reductionist theory. But while the identity theorists reduce mental states to brain states, the behaviorists reduce mental states to behavior. Functionalism, in contrast, does not reduce mental states to either brain states or behavior. In treating mental states as functional states, the functionalist sees mental states as something that *mediates* between inputs and outputs.

IS FUNCTIONALISM A VERSION OF PHYSICALISM?

Before moving on to an assessment of functionalism, there's one further issue to which we should attend, namely, how best to classify functionalism with respect to the dualist-physicalist dichotomy. When we first encounter it, the theory may seem to transcend this dichotomy, offering a genuinely third way. But on closer examination, it seems likely that functionalism can be slotted in to our traditional framework.

On first thought, functionalism may seem to be a version of **physicalism**. Unlike the identity theory, functionalism would not be a version of type physicalism, but it's natural to see it as a version of token physicalism – and indeed, that's how many functionalists cast themselves. Though very different types of states may all be instances of the same functional type, if they are all physical states of some type or other, then **token physicalism** will be true.

But now a further question arises: why couldn't a non-physical state play the same functional role as a physical state? Consider some non-physical creature like a ghost. Since all that matters for a functionalist attribution of mental states is that the states match the appropriate functional specification, then it looks like the functionalist would have to attribute mentality to any system whose states are appropriately functionally organized – even if that system is not made of matter. Granted, it might be the case in the world as it is that every state capable of playing the functional role associated with the belief that it is raining, or with pain in one's big toe, turns out to be a physical state of some type or other. But that doesn't mean that there couldn't in theory be some non-physical state that plays that functional role. Thus, even though many functionalists themselves pledge allegiance to physicalism, strictly speaking the view seems to be compatible with **dualism**.

ASSESSING FUNCTIONALISM: CONSIDERATIONS IN FAVOR

MULTIPLE REALIZABILITY AND INTERDEFINABILITY

The machine table for the coin press machine has two features that prove to be very important. First, it specifies the functioning of the machine without making any reference to what the machine is made of. Second, the states in the machine table make reference to one another. The specification of S1 makes reference to S2, and vice versa. Both of these features transfer over to the functionalist analysis of mental states.

The first feature enables functionalism to treat mental states as multiply realizable. Functionalists take this aspect of their theory to give them an advantage over the identity theory. Recall our discussion of multiple realizability from Chapter Three. Suppose someone were to be involved in a car accident that caused injury to her brain. It seems plausible that even if her c-fibers were replaced with synthetic substitutes, she would still be able to experience pain sensations after the accident. Pain, in other words, seems to be the kind of state that can be realized in multiple kinds of substances. Though the identity theorist, who equates pain with c-fiber firing, cannot account for this, the functionalist can. For the functionalist, if the synthetic substitute plays the same functional role that the c-fiber previously played, then the accident victim can be in the same kinds of pain states after the accident that she was in before it.

The second feature enables functionalism to treat mental states as interdefinable. Functionalists take this aspect of their theory to give them an advantage over behaviorism. As we saw above, the behaviorist has trouble explaining why, in some cases, a person who is in pain does not cry out, or say "ouch," or exhibit any of the other characteristic pain behaviors. In contrast, the functionalist has an easy explanation here. For the functionalist, the output you produce when you get a painful input depends partly on what other mental states you are in. If you have a strong desire to be stoic, then you might not produce any behavior at all. Likewise if you have the belief that you are in an environment where one shouldn't make any noise. In other words, the mental state of pain is defined at least partly in terms of other mental states like beliefs and desires. In this way, the fact that the functionalists see mental states as interdefinable allows them to account for mental states even when there is an absence of appropriate behavior.

TWO FURTHER ADVANTAGES

Two further advantages are often thought to accrue to functionalism. First, it fits nicely with our practices of attributing mental states to others, what is sometimes called the *problem of other minds*. When you meet someone new, you generally make judgments about whether they are in pain, or have beliefs and desires, without checking to see whether they have a biological brain, let alone without checking anything about which particular neurons are firing. This doesn't show that mental states can't be brain states. But it does suggest that the physicalist view of the **metaphysics** of mental states – what they are – is out of step with the **epistemology** of mental states – how we know about the mental states of others. On the functionalist view, in contrast, the metaphysical story goes hand in hand with the epistemological story. When mental states are defined at least partly in terms of their output, we have a nice explanation for the fact that we attribute mental states on the basis of this output. This same advantage accrues to behaviorism, of course, but given the other problems with behaviorism, this advantage doesn't count for much.

Functionalism's second advantage stems from its commitment to multiple realizability. Given this aspect of the view, functionalism can accommodate the possibility of artificial intelligence. Even if there are no intelligent species like Heptapods, and even if it turns out that octopus pain is very different from human pain, many philosophers take quite seriously the possibility that researchers might one day be able to create a non-biological machine that has mental states. On a type physicalist view, this would be impossible. And while it might not be ruled out by a dualist view, we might think that the dualist has a hard time explaining how the roboticist created the non-physical mental states. In contrast, since the functionalist theory focuses on functional organization rather than physical constitution, the functionalist does not take the fact that a system is artificial to count against its having mentality. In fact, the need to account for machine mentality was one of the very motivations underlying the development of functionalism. The theory's initial articulation in the 1960s occurred simultaneously with various important breakthroughs in computer science and particularly in artificial intelligence, and it's no coincidence that functionalists often draw on computational analogies in spelling out their position. Though we saw one of these analogies above in our discussion of the machine table, we will discuss them in more detail in Chapter Five.

ASSESSING FUNCTIONALISM: PROBLEMS

As we saw in Chapter Three, accounting for the qualitative aspects of our mental life proved problematic for physicalist theories. Similar worries have been raised with functionalist theories. In this section we will consider two different thought experiments that are commonly raised in objection to functionalism.

THE ABSENT QUALIA OBJECTION

In fact, the **zombie** thought experiment that we considered in Chapter Three poses problems not just for physicalism but for functionalism as well. As the zombies are described by Chalmers, they are both physically and functionally identical to human beings. Your zombie twin is not only a physical duplicate of you – identical to you all the way down to the microphysical level – but is also a functional duplicate of you – in states that play exactly the same functional role as the states that you are in. Yet your zombie twin lacks qualia altogether. But if two beings that are functionally identical can differ with respect to whether they have qualitative states, then functionalism can't adequately account for qualia and thus fails to provide an adequate theory of mind. In this way, the zombie case presents a version of the **absent qualia** objection to functionalism. Whether zombies are really imaginable, however, is a hotly contested issue. For this reason, it will be useful to consider a different scenario to raise the absent qualia objection.

Ned Block offers such a scenario with his example of the homunculi-headed robot. This robot has a body that, from the outside, looks exactly like a regular human body. On the inside, however, things are pretty different. In a hollow cavity inside the head, there's a bank of lights connected to the sensory-input neurons, a set of buttons connecting to the motor-output neurons, a little bulletin board, and a bunch of tiny little humanoid creatures called homunculi. Each homunculus implements one square in your machine table. Since we can describe any functional system with a machine table, functionalism entails that we can capture all of your mental operations by a machine table. Of course, this table would be extremely complex, since your mental operations are significantly more complex than, say, the coin press machine we considered earlier. But each particular square in the machine table will be a simple set of instructions described in terms of various outputs and relations to other squares in the table.

Let's suppose that the card posted on the bulletin board reads G. Now consider one particular homunculus, say h12794. The sole task assigned to this homunculus, a task that only needs to be performed very rarely, is as follows: when the card reads G and light i17 goes on, press button o89 and then change the posted card to M. Homunculus h12795 has a slightly different task: when the card reads G and light i18 goes on, press button o76 and do nothing to the posted card. Each homunculus has a task of similar form. If every homunculus does its job correctly, then the robot's functional organization is exactly like yours and its behavior will thus look exactly like yours – it will respond exactly the way you would in response to a given stimulus.

To implement your entire machine table, there would need to be an awful lot of homunculi. Block proposes we might even need a billion of them. But let's suppose that we were able to set the whole thing up. Would such a robot have qualitative states? When its foot came into contact with a sharp tack, would it actually be in pain?

Probably it's hard to have very clear intuitions about this scenario, especially when it's considered in the abstract. The idea of tiny little humanoids populating a hollow cavity inside a robotic head is pretty strange. And though the scenario itself seems conceptually coherent, it doesn't seem like the sort of thing that could be pulled off in our world, given our physical laws. Recognizing all of this, Block proposes a slightly different version of the scenario. Instead of having the machine table implemented by a billion tiny little humanoids inside, why not have the machine table implemented by a billion people? Suppose we recruit the population of both North and South America, which should give us more than enough people. Obviously, they won't fit in the hollow cavity where the homunculi were located, so they will have to implement the machine table remotely. We can equip them with a little device that displays the information formerly exhibited on the bulletin board, receives signals from the lights, and remotely operates the buttons and changes the display. The human designated 12794 has a remote that operates button o89 while the human designated 12795 has a remote that operates button o76, and so on.

Perhaps we couldn't convince people to participate in this experiment for very long, but suppose we managed to get everyone doing it for at least an hour, and so for that hour we had a system – the robotic body plus the one billion people – that was functionally equivalent to you. Now let's return to the questions we raised earlier: Would such a robotic system have qualitative states? When the robot's foot came into contact with a sharp tack, would it actually be in pain? Block predicts that here the intuitive answer is pretty clear: no. There's at least prima facie doubt that a robotic body operated by a billion people each pushing a button now and then could actually feel anything at all. But if we could have two functionally equivalent systems, one that has qualitative states and one that does not, then functionalism cannot be an adequate theory of mind.

Putting this argument in standard form, we get:

The Absent Qualia Argument:

1   We can conceive of an absent qualia scenario, i.e., a scenario where a system lacking qualitative states is functionally equivalent to a system that has qualitative states.
2   If the absent qualia scenario is conceivable, then it is possible.
3   Therefore, the absent qualia scenario is possible. [From 1,2]
4   If the absent qualia scenario is possible, then functionalism does not adequately account for qualitative states.
5   Therefore, functionalism does not adequately account for qualitative states. [From 3,4]

ASSESSING THE ABSENT QUALIA OBJECTION

When initially presented with the homunculi-headed robot, many people have the strong intuition that it couldn't be conscious. In support of this intuition, the defender of the absent qualia objection might point to a principle regarding consciousness often called the **anti-nesting principle**. Originally put forth by Hilary Putnam (1967), this principle states that no organism that can experience a conscious state such as pain can be decomposed into parts that can individually experience that conscious state. Conscious organisms, in other words, cannot contain other conscious organisms as parts. Consciousness doesn't nest. If the anti-nesting principle weren't true, said Putnam, then we might be led to the absurd consequence that a swarm of bees might be counted as a single pain-feeling entity.

But why is this consequence so absurd? In response to these considerations, functionalists would likely question why we should grant the anti-nesting principle. Though it has been claimed by some of its defenders to be a consequence of **Ockham's Razor**, the thought being that we should not unnecessarily multiply our ascriptions of consciousness (Kammerer 2015; see also Tononi 2012), functionalists are unlikely to find this defense convincing.

This skepticism about the anti-nesting principle directly relates to what's likely the most straightforward response available to the functionalists when confronted with the absent qualia objection, i.e., to simply deny the intuition that the robotic system would lack qualitative states. If we really were to imagine what we were supposed to imagine, then we wouldn't doubt that the robotic system had the same qualitative states that you do. This is a style of response that we've seen before. With respect to Mary the color scientist, for example, some philosophers argue that if we really conceived of Mary as having *all* the physical information about color and not just *lots* of physical information about color, then we wouldn't be inclined to think that Mary learns something when she leaves her black and white room and has her first color experience. Likewise, if we really conceived of the machine table as perfectly capturing your functional organization, and not just approximating or partially capturing it, we wouldn't be inclined to deny that the robot had qualitative states. As strange as it may initially seem, the robotic system really does have qualia. Pursuing this line of response would thus be to deny premise 1.

A second response available to the functionalist, one that also involves denying premise 1, arises from the fact that the two machine tables are realized on dramatically different time scales. Presumably when humans implement the machine table, they will do so much more slowly than your brain does. Perhaps this difference means that the robot is not really functionally identical to you. Block himself notes that the time scale of the system shouldn't matter, claiming that we can easily conceive of alien species who operate on dramatically different time scales. But this response by the functionalist might have more bite if we connect it to the previous response. Perhaps the time scale is not important in and of itself but plays a role in causing the kind of imaginative failure invoked by the functionalist's first response. Compare two systems that both implement the coin press machine table. The first dispenses the pressed coin less than a minute after you insert two Euros, while the second dispenses the pressed coin a week later. From the outside, the second machine will appear to be broken, but it is really working, just super, super slowly. Perhaps we form a similar misimpression when we imagine the robotic system.

Time also plays a role in a third functionalist response to the absent qualia objection – yet another response that involves the denial of premise 1. One might worry that it doesn't make sense to talk of functional equivalence *for an hour*. Some mental states only unfold over a longer time horizon. Unfortunately for the functionalist, however, this objection doesn't have much traction. Take two coin press machines that have just been plugged in and begun operation. After an hour, suppose that one of them is unplugged. The fact that it was in operation only for an hour doesn't seem in any way to threaten the claim that two machines were functionally equivalent for that hour.

A BRIEF ASIDE: DOES FUNCTIONALISM ENTAIL THAT THE UNITED STATES IS CONSCIOUS?

The upshot of the absent qualia objection is that functionalism attributes mentality to entities that it shouldn't, i.e., entities that don't have qualia. Traditionally, this objection was pursued by considering hypothetical systems like the homunculi-headed robot proposed by Ned Block. But more recently, a different example has arisen in philosophical discussion. As suggested by Eric Schwitzgebel (2015), functionalism seems to imply that a complex entity like the United States is conscious.

Two quick notes before we consider the argument. First, Schwitzgebel puts his point in terms of *materialism* not *functionalism*. But for our purposes, it will be easier to consider the argument in functionalist terms, and since it seems clear the kind of view Schwitzgebel has in mind is a functionalist-oriented materialism, construing the argument this way doesn't seem to do much of an injustice to his view. Second, Schwitzgebel himself is neutral on whether his argument constitutes an objection to functionalism or instead provides us with grounds for thinking that the United States is conscious. But since, as he admits, the claim that the United States is conscious is "highly bizarre by folk psychological standards" (p. 1717) we'll here treat it as a reason to worry about functionalism.

According to Schwitzgebel, our ordinary thinking about conscious entities is deeply affected by a prejudice he calls *contiguism* – a prejudice against entities whose parts are spatially discontinuous from one another. On his view, however, such prejudice is entirely unwarranted. To help us see this, he offers descriptions of two different science-fictional creatures: the Sirius supersquid and the Antarean antheads. Both are creatures whose behavior strongly suggests the presence of consciousness but whose neural structures are quite different from human beings. The supersquid brain is distributed throughout its tentacles, of which it has thousands, and the nerves communicate via superfast light signals. Importantly, the supersquid can detach its tentacles from its body. A squid with detached tentacles remains fully cognitively integrated and remains fully in control of all of its parts, both intact and detached. The anthead, which looks something like a woolly mammoth, doesn't have neurons at all:

> Their heads and humps contain not neurons but rather ten million squirming insects, each a fraction of a millimeter across. Each insect has a complete set of minute sensory organs and a nervous system of its own, and the antheads' behavior arises from complex patterns of interaction among these individually dumb insects.

In Schwitzgebel's view, both of these creatures are plausibly viewed as conscious despite the fact that they are not spatially continuous entities (or, in the case of the supersquid, not *always* spatially continuous). Perhaps we're disinclined to view the anthead as conscious because we're tempted to believe in the anti-nesting principle, but as we saw above, it's not clear whether that principle has adequate support. But in the case of both the anthead and the supersquid, we don't seem to have any reason to think that the lack of spatial continuity implies a lack of consciousness.

Once we overcome our contiguist prejudice, we can start to think more seriously about the question of whether the United States is conscious. According to Schwitzgebel, once we evaluate the functional organization of the United States we can see all of the following:

- it is a system with sophisticated information processing and environmental responsiveness
- it is capable of an immense quantity of information transfer among its parts
- it is a goal-directed entity that protects and preserves itself by responding relevantly to opportunities and threats
- it is embedded in a natural and social environment and richly connected to the world beyond

And so on. All of these aspects suggest to Schwitzgebel the strong probability that the United States meets the functionalist specifications necessary for consciousness. Insofar as this strikes us as plausible, we have some further support for the functionalist view. But insofar as this strikes us as an absurd conclusion, one that cannot be tolerated, we have another version of the absent qualia objection – one that, unlike the homunculi-headed robot, does not come to us from the realm of science fiction.

THE INVERTED QUALIA OBJECTION

The homunculi-headed robot scenario discussed above suggests that there could be a system functionally identical to you that lacks qualia. The scenario that we will now consider suggests that there could be a system functionally identical to you that has different qualia. More specifically, the suggestion is that there could be two systems that are functionally identical to one another yet whose qualia are inverted relative to one another. The scenario is usually developed in terms of color qualia, such as the qualitative experience of blue vs. the qualitative experience of yellow, or the qualitative experience of red vs. the qualitative experience of green. Over 300 years ago, the possibility of spectrum inversion was raised by English philosopher John Locke when he wondered whether the color that one person sees when looking at a violet might be the same as the color experience another person sees when looking at a marigold. Locke's discussion of this possibility was not meant to cast doubt on any particular theory of mind. But when philosophers in the 1980s began revisiting the idea of the inverted spectrum, they did so specifically because of the trouble it seems to raise for functionalism.

Consider two women, Jade and Scarlet. Both of them stop their cars when they see a stop sign, reach for the same tomatoes when looking for the ripe ones, and describe American flags as being red, white, and blue. They both would agree that grass is green, and that it's the same color as the Grinch's face. They can accurately sort an Uno deck into four piles by color, and they both think that strawberry lollipops look a lot more like cherry lollipops then they look like lime lollipops. In other words, the ways they react to color are indistinguishable from one another; they seem to be functionally identical in this regard. But the fact that they are functionally identical to one another does not seem to rule out the following possibility: Jade might be having a greenish experience whenever Scarlet is having a reddish experience, and vice versa. While Scarlet has a reddish experience when she looks at ripe tomatoes and a greenish experience when she looks at unripe tomatoes, Jade has a greenish experience when she looks at ripe tomatoes and a reddish experience when she looks at ripe tomatoes. But if this scenario is conceivable, and it's thus possible that there could be two systems that are functionally identical to one another yet whose qualia are inverted relative to one another, then functionalism cannot adequately account for qualitative states.

Putting this line of reasoning in standard form, we get an argument whose structure mirrors the absent qualia argument we just considered:

The Inverted Spectrum Argument:

1 The inverted spectrum scenario is conceivable.
2 If the inverted spectrum scenario is conceivable, then it is possible.

3   Therefore, the inverted spectrum scenario is possible. [From 1,2]
4   If the inverted spectrum scenario is possible, then functionalism does not adequately account for qualitative states.
5   Therefore, functionalism does not adequately account for qualitative states. [From 3,4]

ASSESSING THE INVERTED QUALIA OBJECTION

Like the absent qualia argument, the inverted spectrum argument seems especially vulnerable with respect to its first premise. Can we really conceive of what we're being asked to conceive? Of course, merely raising this question is not enough to defeat the argument. Here the burden of proof seems to lie on the functionalist to explain why something that seems conceivable is not really conceivable. To discharge this burden, the functionalist might try to point out ways that any such spectrum inversion would have to manifest in behavior. Any such manifestations would have to be nuanced; as we have already noted, people who are color inverted with respect to one another like Jade and Scarlet will still use color words the same way. But perhaps one of them might categorize red as a warm shade and green as a cool shade, while one of them might categorize green as a warm shade and red as a cool shade.

More generally, in defending the coherence of the inverted spectrum scenario, the opponent of functionalism might point to several well-established, real-world phenomena that are just as strange – perhaps even stranger – than the inverted spectrum scenario. Take **synesthesia**, for example. When someone has synesthesia, an experience in one sensory modality automatically triggers an experience in a different sensory modality, or an experience with one kind of sensory feature automatically triggers an experience of a different sensory feature. Some synesthetes taste shapes, some hear colors. One especially common type of synesthesia involves the association of individual letters or numbers with certain colors. The number 4 written in black ink on a piece of paper may appear pink, while the number 8 written in black ink may appear blue. It's currently thought that there are as many as 60 different types of synesthesia, and some studies have suggested it may occur in as much as three to five percent of the population. Is the suggestion that someone might have a greenish experience when someone else is having a reddish experience really any stranger than the suggestion that someone might have a greenish experience when they see the number 7? Granted, synesthesia is detectable while color inversion is not, so it does not offer us an example of real-life inversion. But thinking about synesthesia might give us a helpful model on which to base our conceptual exploration of the inverted spectrum scenario.

WEAKENING THE THEORY?

As we have seen, the functionalist has various avenues to explore in responding to these qualia-based objections. But that said, worries of this sort continue to plague functionalism. One option for the functionalist would be to lower their aspirations and retreat to a weaker version of the theory. None of the objections raised show that functionalism is inadequate with respect to non-qualitative states like beliefs and desires. So perhaps functionalism should be seen as offering a theory only of non-qualitative mental states, and we need some supplemental theory for the qualitative mental states. Though many contemporary functionalists continue to embrace a strong version of the theory, there are many other contemporary functionalists who see the weaker version as more promising.

CONCLUDING REMARKS

This chapter has introduced us to the functionalist view, a theory of mind that entered the philosophical scene in the 1960s and continues to enjoy considerable support in the 21st century. As we have seen, functionalism was an outgrowth of two physicalist theories that came before it – behaviorism and the identity theory. By allowing for both the multiple realizability and the interdefinability of mental states, functionalism has been able to avoid many of the problems that plagued these earlier theories. As we have also seen, however, functionalism faces some serious objections stemming from considerations about qualia. Like the physicalist theories we considered in Chapter Three, functionalism faces accusations that it is unable to adequately account for the qualitative aspects of our mental lives.

This chapter completes our survey of the three main theories of mind – dualism, physicalism, and functionalism. Though each of these theories has various things that can be said in its favor, there are also serious problems with each of them. Before moving on to the remaining chapters of the book, readers might want to pause for a moment to take stock of their own views on this issue. Which theory, or version of a theory, do you find most attractive? Why? How would you respond to the objections facing your preferred theory?

FURTHER READING

An early defense of functionalism can be found in Putnam (1960). Fodor (1981) provides an accessible overview of functionalism and many of the objections to it. The homunculi-headed robot objection is developed in Block. The Qin I computing system described by Cixin Liu in his science fiction novel *The Three-Body Problem* provides a similar kind of example.

For a non-technical discussion of synesthesia, see Richard Cytoqic's (1993) *The Man Who Tasted Shapes*. The book is described as a "medical detective adventure." For philosophical and scientific perspectives on the phenomenon, see the essays in *Sensory Blending: On Synaesthesia and Related Phenomena* (Deroy 2017).

The Heptapods discussed earlier in the chapter appear in the 2016 movie *Arrival* directed by Denis Villeneuve. The movie is based on a wonderful short story, "The Story of Your Life," by science fiction author Ted Chiang. In the same collection (Chiang 2002) are several other short stories relevant to philosophy of mind, especially "Understand" and "Seventy-Two Letters." The Greg Egan short stories "Learning to Be Me" and "Closer," both in Egan (1995), provide an interesting exploration of functionalism. Members of the futuristic society depicted in these stories have a neural net computer, what they call a "jewel," implanted in them shortly after birth. The jewel learns to imitate their brains down to the level of individual neurons. When members of the society turn eighteen, their organic brains are removed and destroyed, and control of their body is turned over to the jewel.

MACHINE MINDS

The HAL 9000 computer. C3PO and R2D2. The Iron Giant. The Terminator. Tony Stark's assistants Jarvis and FRIDAY. Baymax from *Big Hero 6*. Science fiction is rife with examples of mechanical systems who seem to be highly intelligent, often more intelligent (in at least some respects) than the humans around them.

But we don't need to look to science fiction to find examples of machines who exhibit highly intelligent behavior, even if just in a relatively narrow domain. In 1996, a chess-playing supercomputer named Deep Blue beat grandmaster Garry Kasparov in a single game. Though Deep Blue lost the six-game match, when the two competitors played again the following year the computer emerged victorious – taking the match by a score of 3½ to 2½ after winning two games, losing one, and taking three games to a draw. In 2011, a machine named Watson competed at *Jeopardy!* against former champions Ken Jennings and Brad Rutter, two of the most successful contestants in the history of the show. In this match, which consisted of two games broadcast on national television, Watson emerged victorious – winning both games and racking up a total of $77,147 compared to Jennings' $24,000 and Rutter's $21,600. Questions answered correctly by Watson ranged in subject from classical music to hedgehogs. In 2016, a program named AlphaGo beat professional player Lee Sedol in a game of Go. While the rules of go are simpler than the rules of chess, the game is played on a much bigger board – 19 by 19 squares in Go vs. 8 by 8 squares in chess – that makes the gameplay considerably more complex. In a game of approximately 150 moves, there are about 10^{360} possible moves.

The emergence of these successful computing systems raises a number of questions about mental lives of machines. In this chapter we will focus on two of these questions. The first half of the chapter explores whether machines can think. To do so, we consider two famous thought experiments – one that provides support for an affirmative answer to the question, and another that provides support for a negative answer to the question. The second half of the chapter explores whether machines can feel, i.e., whether they can have emotions. We'll explore this question in the context of two different philosophical theories of emotions.

But before we turn to these questions, we will briefly consider a more familiar case of non-human mentality: animals. Considering when and why we view non-human organisms as having mental lives will shed some light on the parallel case of machine mentality.

ANIMAL MENTALITY

As surprising as it may sound from the perspective of the 21st century, many philosophers throughout history have denied that animals have minds. Writing in the 17th century, Descartes claimed that animals are mere automata, unable to think or to feel pain, and this seemed to be the majority position at the time. Similar positions were offered by Aristotle, Aquinas, Locke, and Kant. In Aristotle's view, for example, while the human soul has the capacity for nutrition, perception, and mind, the animal soul only has the capacity for nutrition and perception.

Of course, not every historical philosopher took this view. Perhaps one of the most notable dissenters on this issue was David Hume (1738/1978), who famously claimed that animals can think and reason just as humans do. But even late in the 20th century, philosophers such as Donald Davidson (1982) and Stephen Stich (1978) offered arguments suggesting that animals do not have the capacity for thought; in their view, animals lack beliefs altogether.

In the 21st century, however, the question seems less one of *do animals have minds?* and more one of *which animals have minds?* We recognize high levels of intelligence in animals as diverse as birds, dolphins, and the great apes; we recognize interesting communication abilities in animals such as honeybees, chickens, and prairie dogs. Even more significantly, animals such as chimpanzees, orangutans, dolphins, parrots, and border collies have been taught linguistic systems that enable them to communicate (to at least some extent) with humans. Stories of impressive animal feats – feats that seem to hint at sophisticated mental abilities – abound in the internet age. To give just a single example, one story making the rounds in spring 2019 concerns a wild manta ray known by local divers as Freckles. After getting fish hooks stuck near her eyes, Freckles seemed to deliberately seek out a familiar human diver in an effort to request assistance removing them.

But *why* do we think that animals such as these have minds? As laypeople, we likely engage in a kind of implicit analogical reasoning: certain kinds of behavior when produced by humans are the result of beliefs, desires, emotions, and so on, so when we see similar kinds of behavior from animals, it seems to make sense that their behavior too must be produced by beliefs, desires, emotions, and so on. Importantly, scientists studying animals seem increasingly to think that the best explanations for various pieces of animal behavior must invoke folk psychological states such as beliefs, desires, intentions, and so on.

Given our tendency to analogize between our own behavior and animal behavior, one might naturally wonder why we don't seem to have the same tendency to analogize between our own behavior and machine behavior. When we see an animal engaging in a certain kind of avoidance-behavior we attribute fear to it, but when we see a robot engaging in a similar kind of avoidance-behavior we are generally not inclined to explain its actions in the same way. Rather, we simply take the behavior to be the result of the robot's programming. Perhaps this discrepancy comes from the fact that we take animals, unlike the robots, to have similar brains to our own. But of course, many of the animals to which we attribute mental states have brain structures that are vastly different from those of humans, brain structures that often do not even have the same evolutionary lineage. It will be useful to keep these points about animal mentality in mind as we explore the questions of whether machines can think and feel in the remainder of this chapter.

CAN MACHINES THINK?

THE TURING TEST

The 2014 movie *The Imitation Game* depicts the WWII code-breaking efforts of English computer scientist Alan Turing (played by Benedict Cumberbatch) and, in particular, his successful attempt to crack the Nazi Enigma codes. The title is in part a nod to Turing's secret life as a gay man, for which he was later prosecuted by the British authorities. But it is also a nod to his famous 1950 paper, "Computing Machinery and Intelligence." In this paper, Turing laid out an imitation game, now typically referred to as the Turing test, that offers a method for determining whether machines can think.

To introduce his test, Turing first asks us to consider an imitation game involving a man, a woman, and a neutral investigator of any gender. All three participants are in separate rooms. They communicate with one another in writing via what Turing describes as "a teleprinter communicating between the two rooms." Given the advances in technology since the mid-20th century, however, it's probably easier to think of the communication as occurring by email or text. The job of the investigator is to determine which of the two contestants is which, and the woman wins if she is able to successfully fool the investigator into identifying her as the man.

But now suppose we swap out one of the human contestants for a machine. Will the investigator be able to tell which is the human and which is the machine? According to Turing, if the computer is able to fool the investigator into identifying it as human approximately as often as the woman was able to fool the investigator into identifying her as a man, then we should conclude that the machine can think.

The test is deliberately set up to try to eliminate bias against the machine. By keeping the investigator in a separate room from the contestants, the fact that a machine does not look like a human becomes rightly irrelevant. Why should looks matter for whether one can think? Also irrelevant is whether the machine can eat a chocolate bar, run a marathon, or snap its fingers. It doesn't even matter whether the machine has fingers. But again, why should any of this matter for whether one can think? What does matter, says Turing, is how the machine performs in conversation. A conversation can range across a great variety of subjects – from mathematics to the weather, from the analysis of poetry to a debate about the relative merits of two political candidates – and its open-ended nature requires the machine to exhibit capabilities of both breadth and depth.

When first considering the test, it may seem that there are various ways that the machine might be tricked into revealing itself. For example, the investigator might ask the machine its birthday or its parents' names. But just as the woman participating in the imitation game may lie when answering questions, so too can the machine. The machine can also take various other measures that might be necessary to prevent its true identity from being too easily revealed. When asked a complicated mathematical equation such as the multiplication of a five-digit number by a three-digit number, the machine may deliberately pause before giving its answer in an attempt to better approximate the time that it would take a human to answer the question. It also might deliberately make an occasional mistake in an attempt to better approximate the human propensity for error.

At the time Turing published his article, the machines in existence were far too unsophisticated even to attempt this kind of competition; in fact, the field of Artificial Intelligence (AI) had not yet officially been born. But Turing nonetheless predicted that by the end of the 20th century, it would be possible for a machine to fool the investigator and pass the test. His prediction turned out to be false, and even now, twenty years into the 21st century, no computer has yet been successful. But, as is shown by the examples of Deep Blue, Watson, and AlphaGo, machines have been successful at matching or beating human performance on intelligent tasks in more limited domains. Moreover, given the rapidly accelerating sophistication of personal assistant programs such as Siri and Alexa, the day that Turing's prediction comes true does not seem that far off. What conclusion we would then be entitled to draw – whether we should conclude that a machine that passes the Turing test counts as thinking – remains a matter of considerable debate.

When first hearing about the Turing test, people sometimes raise the following worry: isn't the test being unfair to the machine by forcing it to imitate a human? Perhaps a machine could think without thinking in the same manner as a human does, but such a machine would be unable to pass the Turing test. Why should we constrain machine intelligence to a human mold?

The basic point underlying this worry seems like a reasonable one. Even if machines do think, they may do so in a way that is vastly different from the way that humans think. But when the Turing test is properly understood, this worry can be easily set to rest. In proposing this test, Turing means explicitly to avoid the question of how the notion of thinking should be defined. He is not defining thinking as synonymous with human thinking, because he is not providing any definition of thinking at all. Rather, he is offering a way for us to test whether thinking is present.

Importantly, in offering us this test, Turing seems to view himself as offering only a **sufficient condition** for intelligence, not a **necessary condition** for it. Consider the following analogy. To determine whether someone is an American citizen, we might ask them to produce their passport. Anyone who can produce a valid passport issued by the US government is an American citizen, so having such a passport is a sufficient condition for being an American citizen. But there are of course American citizens who cannot produce valid passports issued by the US government. They might have lost their passports or they might never have applied for one in the first place. Having a valid passport issued by the US government is not a necessary condition for being an American citizen. Just as we shouldn't conclude that someone who does not have a valid passport issued by the US government is not an American citizen, we shouldn't conclude that a machine that does not pass the test does not think. If a machine does pass the test, we should conclude that it can think. But if doesn't pass, we shouldn't draw any conclusion at all about its thinking capacity.

THE SEAGULL TEST

Even though we can dispel the worry that the test is humancentric, there is a more sophisticated worry in the vicinity. Philosopher

Robert French (1990) has given voice to this worry by offering an analogy. Suppose a group of philosophers is trying to pin down the essence of flying. They first try the following definition: flying is moving through the air without touching the ground. But that definition shows itself to be problematic, since when a pitcher throws a baseball to home plate, we don't describe the baseball as flying. After trying other definitions, which likewise fail, the philosophers opt for a different strategy. Rather than trying to define what flying is, they decide to focus on an uncontroversial example of something that flies – a seagull, say. Anything that can fool a neutral observer into identifying it as a seagull counts as flying. If something can't fool the observer, if it can't pass the Seagull test, they will withhold judgment altogether.

Lots of things that fail the Seagull test, like baseballs and bullets and soap bubbles, should fail the Seagull test. But there are also lots and lots of things that fail the Seagull test that are wholly uncontroversial examples of flying things. Helicopters, airplanes, and drones will fail. So will bats, bumblebees, hummingbirds, and dragonflies. Given that there are so many different kinds of flying things that won't possibly be able to pass the Seagull test, it starts to seem like a very silly way to test for flying ability. French charges that we should conclude something similar about the Turing test. Just as the Seagull test is really a test about being indiscernible from a seagull and not about flying, the Turing test is really a test about being indiscernible from a human and not about thinking.

ORIGINALITY

In the second half of the paper in which he first proposed his test for thinking, Turing considers nine different objections and aims to answer them. We will here consider two of those objections. The first of these, what Turing calls *Lady Lovelace's objection*, is inspired by some remarks of Ada Lovelace, an English countess and mathematician. In the early 19th century, the English mathematician Charles Babbage worked to develop a machine he called the Analytical Engine, and Lovelace collaborated on its design. (While Babbage may be described as the father of the computer, Lovelace may be described as the first computer programmer.) In describing the Analytical Engine in her memoirs, she noted that "it has no pretensions to *originate* anything" – that it only does what it is told to do. This gives rise to the following objection to the Turing test: the fact that a machine can pass the test shows only that it has good programming, not that it thinks. In order to be counted as thinking, a machine would have to evidence some originality or creativity.

On one way of interpreting this objection, it seems to suggest that the machine would have to do something genuinely new, something never before seen in the world, in order to count as thinking. One might respond as Turing does by noting, as the old saying goes, that there's nothing new under the sun. Moreover, how many of us have done things that are genuinely new? If this is what's required for something to think, then it's probably going to turn out that many of our friends and family members don't count as thinking beings. That seems like a pretty problematic result.

On another way of interpreting this objection, the problem is not that the machine fails to do something genuinely new but rather that it fails to do anything new relative to its programming. Given that everything the machine does is a direct result of what it's been programmed to do, its success at the Turing test shows something only about the intelligence of its programmers. Its performance in the test doesn't show us anything about its own intelligence. This objection seems to have considerable pull on people when they first consider the Turing test. And it does seem true that the machine's output is simply a result of its programming. But on further reflection, we can see that this way of interpreting Lady Lovelace's objection also sets an unreasonably high bar for thinking. Each of us is genetically programmed in all sorts of ways from the moment of conception, and then once we enter the world we are further programmed each and every day by way of our interactions with parents, grandparents, aunts and uncles, babysitters, teachers, and so on. We don't usually call it programming, of course, but how different is it, really? Don't you say "please" when making a request and respond with "you're welcome" when someone thanks you? Don't you cover your mouth when you sneeze and close the door to the stall when using a public restroom? When you enter a classroom, don't you sit in one of the chairs rather than standing in the corner or lying down on the floor? In many ways, both small and significant, our linguistic and behavioral responses have been deeply ingrained by years and years of reinforcement – reinforcement that, once you stop to think about it, looks an awful lot like a machine's programming.

THE ARGUMENT FROM CONSCIOUSNESS

Let's turn to a different objection discussed by Turing, namely, what he calls *the argument from consciousness*. The Turing test judges whether something is thinking on the basis of how it behaves. But as we learned from our discussion of the failure of behaviorism in Chapter Four, we can't identify mental states with behavior. To be a thinker, it's not enough for a system simply to behave as if it's thinking. It matters what's going on inside. Just as a very good actor might fool us into thinking they're in pain when they're not really in pain, the machine might fool us into thinking it's thinking when it's not really thinking. The machine might be a completely unconscious automaton, no more thinking than a rock or a table. Though a thermostat that activates the air conditioning when the temperature reaches 76 degrees Fahrenheit behaves *as if* it thinks that the room is too hot, we don't conclude that it has genuine thoughts about the temperature. Likewise, though a machine that successfully answers the investigator's questions about poetry and mathematics and politics behaves *as if* it thinks about these matters, it's not clear why we should conclude that it has genuine thoughts about them.

This objection is a deep one, and it is probably the most serious objection faced by the Turing test. The problem stems from the fact that there seems to be no way to know exactly what's going on in the machine. We can't know what it's like to be the machine; indeed, we can't even know whether there is anything that it's like to be the machine. But, as Turing notes in response, pushing too hard on this line of objection ends up in a commitment to solipsism, the view that each person can only be certain of the existence of their own mind. Just as I don't know exactly what's going on inside the machine, or whether there's anything really going on inside the machine, I also don't know exactly what's going on inside my neighbors or my children or my students. Since the evidence we have that the machine thinks is exactly the same kind of evidence that we have about the fellow humans that we interact with on a daily basis, Turing thinks it is more reasonable to accept the conclusion that a machine that passes the test is thinking than it is to deny that all of the fellow humans that we interact with on a daily basis are thinking.

Alternatively, in response to this kind of worry, some philosophers have recently suggested that we need to move beyond the Turing test when thinking about machine consciousness. One such philosopher is Susan Schneider (2019), who suggests that determining whether a computer system is conscious might be best understood on analogy with the process of diagnosing a medical illness. When diagnosing a medical illness, doctors will often use more than one test or procedure. Likewise, when attempting to determine whether a machine system is conscious, we might do best to rely on a variety of different methods and markers. In some cases, one method may be more illuminating, while in other cases another method might help us better to assess the situation.

As to the question of what tests in particular might be relevant, Schneider makes several proposals. The first, the AI Consciousness Test (or ACT, for short), aims to determine whether the machine has developed views of its own about consciousness and whether it is reflective about and sensitive to the qualitative aspects of experience. In employing this test, we would first have to make sure that the machine has not been provided with any antecedent information about consciousness. We could then ask the machine various questions designed to see how it conceives of its own mental states, its connection to its physical manifestation, the possibilities for its embodied survival, and so on. Among these questions could be: what is it like to be you right now? Could you survive the permanent deletion of your program? We could even use the machine to test a version of the Knowledge Argument discussed in Chapter Three. For a machine with color processing, we could prevent it from ever seeing red and then, once it is eventually exposed to red things for the first time, we could see how it reacts and how it describes its experiences.

Importantly, Schneider makes clear that passing the ACT should be seen as **sufficient** but not **necessary** for consciousness. Treating it as a necessary condition for consciousness would be to fall victim to the same kind of humancentric bias we earlier worried about in our discussion of the Turing test. Just because humans develop a certain conception of their own consciousness, e.g., that we can imagine ourselves existing apart from our bodies, this doesn't mean that all conscious creatures would develop this same conception. Schneider thus goes on to lay out other tests that can be used in conjunction with the ACT test. To give just one more example, her chip test focuses not on machine behavior but on machine composition. Suppose that there are some pieces of technology that, when integrated into a human brain, seem to support the presence of consciousness. Schneider suggests that if there are machines that utilize this same technology – these same "chips" – then we should be disposed to take seriously the possibility that they are conscious.

Whether any of these particular tests prove viable, they offer interesting alternatives to the Turing test. Indeed, Schneider notes that the ACT in particular has an important advantage over the Turing test. Though both tests focus on behavior, the Turing test does so as part of a deliberate effort to avoid taking on the question of what's going on inside the "mind" of the machine. In contrast,

> ACT is intended to do exactly the opposite: it seeks to reveal a subtle and elusive property of the machine's mind. Indeed a machine might fail the Turing test, because it cannot pass for a human, but it passes an ACT, because it exhibits behavioral indicators of consciousness.
>
> (Schneider 2019, 56)

THE CHINESE ROOM THOUGHT EXPERIMENT

In introducing his test, Turing aimed to provide a basis for an affirmative judgment on the question of whether machines can think. For an alternate view on this question, we turn now to a thought experiment proposed by American philosopher John Searle. In a sense, Searle's thought experiment presents us with a variant of the Argument from Consciousness objection that we just considered. Searle, however, is concerned less with consciousness than with **intentionality**. As we saw in Chapter One, when a mental state has intentionality it is about or aims at some state of affairs in the world. When I think to myself, "The firefighters have contained the wildfire," I am referring to a particular group of people and a particular event – my thought is about them. If I were to write this sentence on a piece of paper, or utter the sentence aloud, those words too would be about that particular group of people and that particular event. But if, by chance, the howling of the wind was to produce noises that sounded just like my utterance, or the swirling of the wind was to produce marks in the sand that looked just like my writing, the wind's howls or swirls would not be about anything. They do not have any intentional content. Searle thinks something similar is true of a machine's mental states and utterances, and, he claims, without intentionality there cannot be genuine thought.

To demonstrate this point, Searle develops what has become known as the Chinese Room thought experiment. The thought experiment requires you to pick a language about which you are entirely ignorant. Searle, a native English speaker, chooses Chinese, but if you have even partial understanding of Chinese or can recognize its characters, you should choose a different language – Arabic or Greek, perhaps. Now suppose that you are locked in a room. (Don't worry: unlike Mary's room, this one allows you access to the full color spectrum.) Inside the room, you are given a giant book consisting of a very long set of instructions. Each instruction has roughly the form, "If you are provided with the input X, produce the output Y," where the Xs and Ys are filled in with a set of characters that are completely unrecognizable to you. They look just like meaningless scribbles. The room has a slot where, from time to time, a piece of paper is sent in to you with some of these unrecognizable characters. Using the giant book, you look up the appropriate instruction for the input you have received and issue the appropriate output through the same slot. As you do this more often, you get better and better at using the giant instruction book so that you can produce the appropriate output quickly, even when pieces of paper start coming in quickly and regularly.

Here's the payoff. Unbeknownst to you, the characters coming in and going out through the slot are actually sentences in Chinese. The rulebook that you've been given is so good the outputs that you've been producing by using it are indistinguishable from the outputs that would be produced by a native Chinese speaker. From outside the room, it seems just as if the room contains a native Chinese speaker. Indeed, it passes the Turing test for Chinese. But now ask yourself this: in such a situation, would you have any understanding of Chinese? Searle thinks the answer to this question is clearly "no".

What you have inside the room is just like what a computer has. Your rulebook is just like a program. Since following a set of rules, even ones that enable you to pass the Turing test for Chinese, cannot provide you with an understanding of Chinese, Searle concludes that the same would be true for a computer. Even if a computer were able to pass the Turing test for Chinese, the mere instantiation of a program is unable to provide it with actual understanding of Chinese.

Searle often summarizes this reasoning with roughly the following argument:

The Chinese Room Argument:

1   Computer programs are formal (syntactic).
2   Human minds have mental contents (semantics).
3   Syntax by itself is not sufficient for semantics.
4   Thus, programs are not sufficient for minds.

When providing a specification of a language, we can do so syntactically or semantically. A syntactic specification – the language's syntax – tells us what words and symbols belong to the language and gives us rules for how those words and symbols can be permissibly combined. Grammatical rules that tell us that certain kinds of words (e.g., nouns) can be followed by certain other kinds of words (e.g., verbs) would fall into the syntactic specification. A semantic specification – the language's semantics – tells us what those words and symbols mean. While the first two premises of the argument are largely definitional, the third premise is meant to be established by the Chinese Room thought experiment. From these premises, Searle concludes that the instantiation of a syntactic program is not enough to provide a computer with understanding. In other words, running a program – even a very, very good program, even one that enables a computer to pass the Turing test – will never enable a computer to think.

THE SYSTEMS REPLY

Searle's paper introducing the Chinese Room thought experiment was published in 1980 in an interdisciplinary journal, *Brain and Behavioral Sciences*. This journal has a policy of open peer commentary, where colleagues from various disciplines in cognitive science respond to each published paper. Searle's article was followed by twenty-seven critiques from philosophers, psychologists, neuroscientists, and AI researchers, among others. Despite these criticisms, Searle closed his response to the commentary with assurance: "I conclude that the Chinese room has survived the assaults of its critics." Moreover, even though considerable literature has since been devoted to criticizing the Chinese Room argument, Searle has persisted in affirming its conclusiveness. As he notes in a paper that was published on the tenth anniversary of the original article, "the debate has raged on for ten years and still continues. Though many interesting points have emerged, I think the original argument is quite decisive."

Many philosophers disagree with Searle's assessment of the success of the argument and the thought experiment on which it is based. One common line of attack suggests that Searle is looking for understanding in the wrong place. Suppose a bank has a vault with a three-digit combination lock. On the advice of a security firm, no single employee at the bank is trusted with the whole three-digit combination. The bank manager knows only the first number of the combination, an assistant bank manager knows only the second number, and another assistant bank manager knows only the third number. Though none of these employees can be said to know the combination, they can unlock it as a group. In other words, there is an overarching system, a system of which each of the three employees is a part, that knows the combination. Similarly, though you may not understand Chinese while in the Chinese Room, you are simply one part of a bigger system, and it's the bigger system that understands Chinese.

Searle finds this reply unpersuasive. In the original Chinese Room setup, the system is constituted by you plus the rulebook. Searle suggests that you might memorize the rulebook such that you become the whole system in its entirety. There is no system distinct from you. But even having memorized the rulebook you still won't understand Chinese.

According to the proponent of the systems reply, however, the relationship between systems and parts of systems might be a little bit more complex than that. You might not know how to do protein synthesis, but there is a part of you that does, namely, your digestive tract. It has the relevant know-how. The system of which you are a part – a system that isn't distinct from you – understands how to do something even though you don't. Likewise, in the Chinese Room, the system of which you are a part – a system that isn't distinct from you – can have understanding even if you don't.

THE LUMINOUS ROOM

To flesh out the systems reply, we might usefully consider a parallel thought experiment offered by Paul and Patricia Churchland. Suppose you were placed inside a dark room with a large bar magnet. Now wave the bar around as hard as you can. Will the luminance of the room change? Most people have the intuition that no matter how much work you put into your efforts, the room will remain dark. From this, we might derive the claim that forces are insufficient for luminance. If we put this claim to work in an argument parallel to Searle's, we could reach the conclusion that electricity and magnetism – which are forces – are not sufficient for luminance. But, as was first proposed by James Clerk Maxwell in 1864, light is indeed an electromagnetic force.

According to the Churchlands, consideration of this parallel thought experiment helps us to see what's wrong with Searle's Chinese Room thought experiment. In the luminous room, there is indeed luminance. It's just far too low to be detectable by the human inside the room: "Given the low frequency with which the man can oscillate the magnet, the wavelength of the electromagnetic waves produced is far too long and their intensity is much too weak for human retinas to respond to them." There is light in the system, even though the human inside the room can't detect it. Likewise, as the Churchlands would urge us to conclude, there can be understanding in the Chinese Room system, even though the human inside the room can't detect it.

THE ROBOT REPLY

Although there are several other common replies to the Chinese Room argument, we will here consider just one more. According to the robot reply, the reason that there is no understanding in the Chinese Room is that the system has no way to connect its inputs and outputs to the world. It lacks sensory apparatuses. A better candidate for a machine with understanding would be a robotic system with arms and legs that enabled it to move and audio-visual cameras that enabled it to take in data from the world. The robot's core processor would not just perform operations on formal symbols but would also control all of the movements of the robot. In this case, says the proponent of the robot reply, the robot would be able to have genuine mental states with intentional content.

Searle is no more persuaded by the robot reply than he was by the systems reply. In an attempt to show that it is unsuccessful, he suggests a modification to the original Chinese Room scenario. It might be that the entire room that you are in is somehow con-nected to a robot body. Some of the symbols might come in via the audiovisual cameras and some of the symbols that you send out might result in movements to the robotic arms and legs. Still, says Searle, from your perspective inside the room, you are still just manipulating symbols. Though the robotic video cameras might be in contact with a cat, and thereby the symbols that come into the room refer to that cat, all of that is completely lost on you. For you, those symbols don't mean "cat." They don't mean anything at all. Even though this system interacts with the outside world, the system's inner processes are still solely syntactic ones. In Searle's view, there is no way for the system to bridge the gap from syntax to semantics.

THE CHINESE ROOM AND FUNCTIONALISM

Before moving on from the Chinese Room, it will be worth explicitly taking up one question that often comes up in this con-text: does the Chinese Room argument present an objection to **functionalism**? In his original paper, Searle's explicit target was not functionalism but Strong AI, a particular branch of Artificial Intelligence research. Unlike Weak AI, which uses the computer as a research tool, developing programs as a way to test theories about mental processes, Strong AI is itself a theory about mental pro-cesses. On this view, human intelligence results from the brain's instantiation of some sort of program, and thus a machine could achieve intelligence in virtue of its instantiation of a program.

Both Strong AI and functionalism are motivated by a basic computational analogy – that the mind is to the brain as a computer's software is to its hardware. But the theories are not identical. Though functionalism is consistent with the possibility of an appropriately programmed machine having mental states, the functionalist's theory lays down specific requirements on what will count as an appropriate program. In particular, it will matter whether the programmed computer is in the same sorts of functional states as a human being.

This point helps us to see that, even if Searle's Chinese Room argument is successful against Strong AI, functionalism may escape unscathed. In the Chinese Room thought experiment, the system passes the Turing test and is thus behaviorally indistinguishable from a native Chinese speaker. But functionalism is not behaviorism. What matters for the functionalist theory is not just what the behavior of the system is but what its functional organization is. Insofar as the Chinese Room system does not share the same functional organization as a native Chinese speaker, the functionalist has a good explanation for why understanding would not be present in such a system.

CAN MACHINES FEEL?

Having considered at some length the question of whether machines can think, we turn now to another important question about the possible mental life of machines: can they feel?

AN ANSWER FROM SCIENCE FICTION

Though thinking machines are a staple in the science fiction literature, such machines tend not to be portrayed as having the capacity to feel. What's perhaps the standard science fiction approach to machine feelings is captured in an exchange between two machines, Frost and Mordel, from Roger Zelazny's short story, "For a Breath I Tarry." Frost and Mordel live in a future in which humankind has become extinct, and Mordel is trying to explain to Frost the difference between humans and machines. Mordel first tries to explain to Frost the difference between measuring coldness, something machines can do, and feeling coldness, something that machines cannot do. Frost remains unconvinced. "If I were aware of the point in a temperature-scale below which an object is cold to a Man and above which it is not, then I, too, would know cold." Mordel disagrees, telling Frost that this would just be another form of measurement. "But given sufficient data," replies Frost, I could obtain the conversion factor which would make me aware of the condition of matter called 'cold'." Here again Mordel denies that this would be to *know* cold. In such a case, Frost would be aware of the existence of cold, but not aware of coldness itself. When Frost claims not to understand, Mordel offers a more detailed explanation:

> I told you that Man possessed a basically incomprehensible nature. His perceptions were organic; yours are not. As a result of His perceptions He had feelings and emotions. These often gave rise to other feelings and emotions, which in turn caused others, until the state of His awareness was far removed from the objects which originally stimulated it. These paths of awareness cannot be known by that which is not-Man. Man did not feel inches or meters, pounds or gallons. He felt heat, He felt cold; He felt heaviness and lightness. He *knew* hatred and love, pride and despair. You cannot measure these things. *You* cannot know them. You can only know the things that He did not need to know: dimensions, weights, temperatures, gravities. There is no formula for a feeling. There is no conversion factor for an emotion.

Of course, there are some feeling machines in science fiction, even if it's not the norm. Marvin, the super-intelligent robot from the *Hitchhiker's Guide* series, not only experiences emotions but also suffers from deep and unrelenting depression. Data, the 24th-century android from *Star Trek: The Next Generation*, is unable to experience emotions when equipped with his original positronic brain but eventually is able to do so with the addition of a special "emotion chip" designed by his creator, a master cyberneticist. Interestingly, however, when a science fiction machine develops the ability to experience emotions, the story often considers the machine to have "transcended" its machineness. After Frost transfers the matrix of his awareness to an artificially grown human body and then finally experiences fear, the other machines proclaim him to be human – in the words of Mordel, "Frost is a Man."

All this said, the question we're now considering, the question of whether machines can feel, can hardly be settled philosophically based on the negative answer supported by science fiction. Rather, this brief look at the machines of science fiction simply suggests how deep our intuitions run on the matter. Though we find it easy to imagine thinking machines, we seem to find it much harder to imagine feeling machines – even in the fantastic, futuristic worlds portrayed by science fiction authors. As we now turn to philosophical theories of emotions, we will see to what extent these pre-theoretic intuitions hold up and to what extent they do not.

WHAT ARE EMOTIONS?

The term "feeling" captures at least two different kinds of mental states: bodily sensations, like pains and itches, and emotions, like fear and anger. We often use the term "feeling" to capture moods as well. Emotions and moods, both of which are referred to as *affective states*, seem closely related to one another. Someone entering an abandoned house might be scared about what they're going to find when they open the cellar door, or they might just be in a generally fearful mood. Whether emotions and moods should be classified together or treated as two different kinds of mental states is a matter of considerable dispute. Some philosophers think the difference is simply a matter of degree; others think that it is a difference in kind. However this question is to be settled, here we will focus simply on emotions.

Emotions are typically differentiated into about six to eight general categories. One particularly common classification owes to 20th-century emotion researcher Paul Ekman. On Ekman's scheme, the basic emotions fall into six types: anger, disgust, fear, happiness, sadness, and surprise. Another 20th-century psychologist, Robert Plutchik, suggests that we can arrange and categorize emotions diagrammatically in a circular shape. Going clockwise from the top, the eight basic emotions on Plutchik's "wheel of emotion" are joy, trust, fear, surprise, sadness, disgust, anger, and anticipation. Interestingly, these characterizations do not differ very much from one proposed by Chinese thinkers as far back as the second century BC. In the seventh book of the *Book of Rites*, an ancient Chinese text that's at the core of the Confucian canon, emotions are classified into seven different basic types: joy, anger, sadness, fear, love, disliking, and liking. In addition to these basic emotions, there are also numerous complex emotions such as guilt, jealousy, shame, and pride. Though basic emotions tend to occur more or less automatically, complex emotions are more likely to result from cultural conditioning or previous associations. To give just one example, whether you feel ashamed when you let out a burp after a meal will likely depend on whether you have been raised in a country in which it is considered rude or a country in which it is considered a sign of appreciation.

Emotions tend to be described along three different dimensions. Emotional *valence* concerns whether the emotion is positive or negative. An emotion's *intensity* concerns how strongly it is felt. Finally, an emotion's *arousal measure* concerns how calming or exciting it is. While the valence of an emotion doesn't change, its intensity and arousal measure will vary from emotional episode to emotional episode. The joy someone feels when finding a quarter on the sidewalk might be relatively low in both intensity and arousal measure, especially in comparison to the joy that same person feels when discovering they have a winning Powerball lottery ticket.

Generally speaking, emotions are thought to be relatively short lasting. They tend not to last longer than just a few minutes, and they may even last for just a few seconds. Emotions are also thought to be **intentional** states. When you're fearful or angry, there's some particular thing – be it a person, an object, or an event – at which your fear or anger is directed.

EMOTIONS AS BODILY RESPONSES

With this general picture of emotions before us, we can now explore two common theories of emotion. The first, what we'll call **the bodily response theory**, was developed in the late 19th century by two different thinkers, William James (1884, 1890) and Carl G. Lange (1885/1922), working independently from one another. On this view, emotions consist in the recognition of a collection of bodily responses that result from certain situations, with each emotion defined by a different set of such bodily responses. Suppose you're hiking and you see a rattlesnake, coiled to strike, on the trail in front of you. Your heart starts to beat faster, your blood pressure rises, you breathe more quickly, various stress hormones are released, and your body starts to shake. For James and Lange, it's your recognition of all of these bodily reactions that constitutes your fear. Or suppose that you have just returned from a long hiking trip when you are effusively greeted by your Labrador retriever. In this case, your brain releases dopamine and serotonin, your heart rate lowers, the corners of your mouth start to tug upwards, and so on. For James and Lange, it's your recognition all of these bodily reactions that constitutes your joy.

In ordinary talk, we are likely to think of bodily reactions as being a result of emotions. We might think that we cry because we feel sad, or that we smile because we feel joyful. On the bodily response theory, however, this way of thinking would be a mistake. To use an example of James, it's not that we tremble because we feel fear, but rather that we feel fear because we are trembling. Our emotions are not the cause of our bodily reactions but rather are constituted by them.

Though the bodily response theory remains popular even today, it faces several significant objections. First, given that the theory tries to distinguish emotions from one another on the basis of bodily responses, it is threatened by the fact that several different emotions seem to have very similar bodily response profiles. How different are the bodily reactions of fear from the bodily reactions of anger, for example? Second, the theory seems unable to account for the intentionality of emotions. How can we explain the difference between my fear of a rattlesnake and my fear of a lion simply on the basis of my bodily responses? Finally, we might wonder whether certain emotions could be felt even in the absence of the relevant bodily responses. Mightn't you feel fear even without a racing heartbeat and trembling hands? Contemporary philosophers who offer versions of the bodily response theory generally make various modifications to the theory in an effort to avoid these objections, but not everyone agrees that they can successfully do so.

MACHINES AND THE BODILY RESPONSE THEORY

The truth of the bodily response theory of emotions could go a long way towards explaining our intuitive sense that machines cannot have emotions. If machines lack bodies, then they cannot experience the bodily responses that constitute emotions. And even in cases where they do have robotic bodies, if those bodies lack hearts and pulses and hormones, then emotions will be impossible for them. This theory could also help to explain why it's only via the acquisition of an organic body that science fiction machines like Frost can experience emotions.

Of course, even when machines do have bodies, if their bodies do not function similarly enough to how humans do, they may not have genuine emotional responses. This premise underlies the polygraph-like Voight-Kampff device employed in *Blade Runner* and its sequel *Blade Runner 2049* to identify artificial humans, the replicants. Someone taking the test is presented with a set of emotionally provocative scenarios. As this is going on, the Voight-Kampff device measures bodily functions such as respiration, heart rate, and barely detectable eye movements such as contractions of the iris muscle. The bodily responses of replicants are subtly different from the bodily responses of humans.

All of this said, however, nothing about the bodily response theory definitively rules out the possibility that machines can have emotions. If a machine is appropriately embodied, and thus can have the appropriate kinds of bodily responses, the machine may well be capable of experiencing emotions. Moreover, the kind of body required would not necessarily have to be an organic body. Absent further argumentation, we have no reason to deny emotions to machines who have mechanical or inorganic bodies that were in states functionally equivalent to beating hearts and racing pulses.

EMOTIONS AS JUDGMENTS

The bodily response theory views emotions as fundamentally non-cognitive. In contrast, the second theory we will consider, *the judgment theory*, views emotions as fundamentally cognitive. On the judgment theory, which has been developed by philosophers such as Robert Solomon (1976) and Martha Nussbaum (2001), we experience emotions when we make certain kinds of judgments or appraisals of the world. Anger, for example, consists in the judgment that you have been wronged or offended in some way, while envy consists in the judgment that someone else has something that you lack and that you desire. Granted, not every time we make a judgment will we experience an emotion. Someone might judge that there's no more milk in the refrigerator, or that it's half past three in the afternoon, without having any kind of emotional experience whatsoever. The judgment theorists thus have to explain the difference between judgments that constitute emotions and those that do not. There are several different kinds of explanations typically offered. Some specify more precisely the content of the judgment involved, while some specify more precisely the nature of the judgment involved.

Just like the bodily response theory, the judgment theory faces several serious objections. First, in identifying emotions with judgments, the theory might seem to overintellectualize things. Infants and animals may be unable to make judgments, but they still seem capable of experiencing emotions. Second, there may be cases in which people experience recalcitrant emotions even when they haven't made the relevant judgments. Someone might know full well that the Grand Canyon skywalk – a cantilevered bridge made of glass – is safe to walk on yet still experience fear when they walk out onto it. Someone might know full well that their spouse has no romantic inclinations towards a co-worker yet still feel a twinge of jealousy when the spouse and co-worker go out on a business lunch.

MACHINES AND THE JUDGMENT THEORY

At least on the face of it, machines seem to make judgments all the time. This seems to hold true even for relatively simple machines, such as the electronic thermostat attached to your air conditioning system. The thermostat makes frequent judgments about the temperature in the room (how else would it know when to turn on the air conditioning?). The point seems even more obvious when it comes to more complex machines. Think of the dialogue box that opens up on your computer indicating that you are running low on hard drive space or that a new operating system update is available. And the same point goes for our smart phones and tablets and even for apps. Doesn't Instagram judge that you need to give it access to your camera roll in order for it to have full functionality? Doesn't the Weather Channel app make a judgment about where you are located before it shows you the current forecast? When you say "Hey Siri" and get a response, isn't that because the app judged that you were talking to it?

Yet even if these kinds of behaviors are indeed appropriately described as machine judgments, this doesn't quite settle the question of whether the judgment theory of emotions is committed to saying that machines can have the emotions. The further question that needs to be settled is whether machines can make the kinds of judgments that are relevant for the experience of emotions. Perhaps your phone can judge that you have failed to update the operating system for several weeks, but can it judge that your failure is causing it moral harm? Can it judge that someone else has just updated their phone's operating system, something that it desires for itself? Given that these are the kinds of judgments that the judgment theory deems necessary for anger and envy, it's these kinds of judgments that a machine would have to be capable of in order for the judgment theory to attribute emotions to it.

Though it seems unlikely that current machines make these kinds of judgments, it does not seem that it would be in principle impossible for them to do so. Thus, as was the case with the bodily response theory, nothing about the judgment theory definitively rules out the possibility that machines can have emotions.

A TEST FOR MACHINE EMOTIONS

As we have seen, it is compatible with both the bodily response theory and the judgment theory that machines could have genuine emotions. At this point, then, a further question arises: how could we tell? Is there an analog to the Turing test when it comes to emotions?

Insofar as suspicions are often raised that a machine could pass the Turing test for thinking just by faking it, without having genuine intelligence, there are likely to be even more suspicions that a machine could pass a Turing test for emotions just by faking it, without having genuine emotions. But it might still be useful to think about the kinds of behavioral responses we would want to see from a machine in order for the attribution of emotions to be even a possibility. In her work on affective computing, Rosalind Picard (1997) has laid out a series of questions that are useful in this regard:

1   Does a person observing the machine describe its behavior with emotional adjectives? For example, would the observer describe the machine's retreating behavior in terms of fear or its lingering behavior in terms of affection?
2   Does the machine respond quickly to threats or other urgent situations? Does it mobilize its resources to respond to these situations appropriately?
3   Does the machine have the capability to predict what kind of responses it would be likely to have in various situations, and does it label those responses in terms of emotional adjectives?
4   Does the machine issue reports on its own internal states? Does it have sensors capable of discriminating different internal states relative to the kind of behavior it is producing? For example, do the sensors differentiate the internal state it is in when it is retreating from the internal state it is in when it is lingering?
5   Is the machine more likely to retrieve, learn, and recognize positive information when it is in a positive internal state than when it is in a negative internal state?

In Picard's view, when the answer to all five of these questions is yes, the machine can be said to have emotions.

THE RELATIONSHIP BETWEEN THINKING AND EMOTION

In the discussion of this chapter thus far, we have separated the question "can a machine think?" from the question "can a machine feel?" and we have explored them independently. Doing so, however, has glossed over one important issue. Many contemporary researchers believe that thinking and feeling do not, indeed *cannot*, typically occur in isolation from one another. Perhaps the best-known proponent of this view is the neuroscientist Antonio Damasio. According to Damasio, emotions play a critical role in decision making and rational thought. Damasio defends this claim by consideration of various individuals who have sustained injuries to the parts of the brain associated with emotional experience. Along with a reduced capacity to experience emotion, such individuals often manifest significant difficulties in their practical reasoning capacities.

Consider what happens when someone is in a scary situation and experiences fear, as when they're confronted with a rattlesnake on the hiking trail right in front of them. As part of experiencing the fear, the individual's attention becomes fully focused on the danger and, more importantly, on what's relevant for avoiding it. Absent the emotion, one becomes simply a cold observer, noticing all of the different aspects of the situation, even the irrelevant ones, and weighing all of the different possible courses of action, even the unhelpful ones. Without emotions to help guide actions, individuals find themselves paralyzed when they have to make decisions, even mundane decisions such as which color folders to use when filing away paperwork and invoices or which brand of shampoo to purchase. Their inability to adequately judge alternatives also makes them unusually risk-prone. Absent emotions, in other words, individuals behave irrationally in many important respects. Thus, while too much emotion may well be detrimental to our reasoning capacities, too little emotion can be equally detrimental (see Picard 1997, Ch. 13).

The interplay between thinking and feeling thus has important consequences for the possibility of machine mentality. Perhaps the connection between reason and emotion that has been found in humans is not a constitutive one, that is, perhaps it is possible in principle to be a fully functioning reasoner without experiencing any emotions whatsoever. But if the connection between reason and emotion is not merely an incidental fact about human reasoning and human emotion, then it might well be a mistake to try to assess machine mentality by separately assessing machine thinking and machine feeling.

CONCLUDING REMARKS

As we continue to develop increasingly sophisticated computer systems — systems that respond to our verbal commands with apparent understanding, systems that advise us how to navigate our roads and even drive our cars for us — the question of machine mentality becomes increasingly salient. Importantly, the question is not merely a theoretical one. If the machines that we're interacting with can think and feel, then we likely have all sorts of moral obligations to them.

As the discussion of this chapter has shown, it's hard to know exactly how we might settle the question of machine mentality.

But before too long the question may well be settled for us. An increasing number of artificial intelligence researchers think we are growing ever closer to what's known as **the Singularity**, the point at which there is such a massive explosion of technological growth that computing systems will be not just intelligent but super-intelligent, achieving a level of sophistication that far surpasses human-level capabilities. Estimates vary wildly as to how close we are to this point. But just to note one concrete estimate: inventor and futurist Ray Kurzweil, in his book called *The Singularity is Near* (2006), predicts that we will achieve this point by 2045.

FURTHER READING

Many papers relevant to the main discussion of this chapter – including Turing (1954) and Searle (1980) – have been anthologized in Margaret Boden's *The Philosophy of Artificial Intelligence* (1990). The "mathematical game" described by Russian author Anatoly Dneprov in a short story originally published in 1961 presents a scenario that seems to anticipate some of the ideas behind Searle's Chinese Room thought experiment. In Dneprov's story, the 1400 members of the Soviet Congress of Young Mathematicians play a game in which, unbeknownst to them, they end up producing a Portuguese sentence despite the fact that none of them speak Portuguese.

Deigh (2009) provides a useful overview of philosophical theories of emotion. Damasio (1994), which is written for the layperson, presents an extended argument for the importance of emotion and its interconnection with reason. Picard (1997) offers an extended exploration of the possibility of machine emotions.

For a helpful overview of issues relating to animal mentality, see Andrews (2015). For a philosophically-oriented discussion of the performance of the AlphaGo system, see Koch (2016).

As suggested by the discussion of this chapter, the topic of machine mentality has proved to be useful fodder for science fiction – both on the page and on the screen. In addition to the films and television shows already men-tioned in the chapter, readers interested in these issues might want to watch the 1968 film *2001: A Space Odyssey*, directed by Stanley Kubrick. This classic film introduces HAL, a computing system that seems to exhibit both intelligence and emotion. Another excellent choice is the 2014 film *Ex Machina*, directed by Alex Garland. Not only does the movie discuss the

Turing test, but it also explicitly references several of the philosophical thought experiments discussed in this book such as the Chinese Room and Jackson's Mary case (see Chapter Three). Two other fairly recent movies that raise interesting issues about machine mentality are *Robot and Frank* (2012) and *Her* (2013). Other works of fiction that take up these issues include Isaac Asimov's novella *Bicentennial Man*; many of the short stories in Asimov's collections *I, Robot* and *Robot Visions* (I recommend "Evidence" in particular); Kurt Vonnegut's "Epicac"; and Brian Aldiss's "Who Can Replace a Man."

THE FUTURE OF THE MIND

In the future world imagined by Ann Leckie in her novel *Ancillary Justice* (2013), not only do there exist conscious machines, but these conscious machines have consciousness that is widely distributed. The book follows the story of *Justice of Toren*, the massive starship whose consciousness extends throughout thousands and thousands of bodies. At one point in the story, the starship describes one moment in her existence when a new body, what they call a *segment*, is about to be connected in to her network, a description that allows us a brief window into what distributed consciousness might be like:

> The tech medic went swiftly to work, and suddenly I was on the table (I was walking behind Lieutenant Awn, I was taking up the mending Two Esk had set down on its way to the holds, I was laying myself down on my small, close bunks, I was wiping a counter in the decade room) and I could see and hear but I had no control of the new body and its terror raised the heart rates of all One Esk's segments. The new segment's mouth opened and it screamed and in the background it heard laughter. .... The segment gasped and sobbed for what seemed like forever and I thought maybe it was going to throw up until...the connection clocked home and I had control of it. I stopped the sobbing.
>
> (Leckie 2013, 170–1)

The world of science fiction is filled with countless other examples of mind-stretching technology. In the *Harry Potter* series, characters such as Albus Dumbledore store some of their memories externally in a device called the Pensieve. These memories are available not only to the person whose memories they are, but to others as well. In William Gibson's cyberpunk classic "Johnny Mnemonic," a story later made into a film, the titular character (played by Keanu Reeves) has a chip implanted in his brain that allows him to store top-secret data for clients. In the 2014 film *Transcendence*, the scientist Will Caster (played by Johnny Depp) uploads his mind to the internet shortly before his body succumbs to poisoning from the polonium-laced bullet that he was shot with during an attack by an anti-technology terrorist group.

Though at this point in the 21st century these examples remain confined to the realm of science fiction, we might wonder whether any of them will one day cross over into the world of science fact. We saw in Chapter Five that the inventor and futurist Ray Kurzweil predicts that the **Singularity**, the point in our technological development at which machine intelligence exceeds human intelligence, will occur by 2045. Kurzweil also predicts that an individual will be able to upload their mind to a computer or android body via a straightforward scan-and-transfer procedure sometime in the late 2030s.

In Chapter Five we explored questions relating to current and future technology by looking at the mental life of machines. In this chapter, we turn to questions relating to current and future technology by thinking about how that technology might affect our own mental life. We explore three potential technological applications that would enable us to extend and enhance our mental capacities: mind extensions, mind uploads, and mind mergers. Exploring these issues will not only shed light on the theories of mind that we considered earlier in this book but will also raise some deep and important questions about the shape and scope of human mentality.

MIND EXTENSIONS

How many phone numbers do you have committed to memory? If you're at all like me, the answer is very few. But there's a sense in which I might be said to know many more phone numbers than the ones that I've committed to memory, for I have a very long list of contacts stored in my cell phone. Do I *literally* know these numbers? According to an influential argument presented by Andy Clark and David Chalmers in their paper, "The Extended Mind," the answer may well be yes (1998). In their view, the mind extends outward into the world, beyond the boundaries of our skin, in cases where we have a special kind of reliance on non-biological devices.

VARIETIES OF EXTERNALISM

Clark and Chalmers' claim that the mind extends out into the world is best understood against the backdrop of the philosophical tradition known as **externalism** (also called anti-individualism). In a paper from the 1970s that has since become highly influential, Hilary Putnam argued that the meanings of certain terms have an externally-oriented component (1975). His argument was based on a thought experiment involving Twin Earth, a world just like ours except for the fact that the stuff that they call "water," the clear, odorless watery stuff that makes up their lakes and rivers and comes out of their faucets, has a different chemical constitution from the stuff we call "water" on earth. While our water is composed of H_2O, their water is composed of XYZ. To the casual observer, H_2O and XYZ are indistinguishable from one another. Consider Oscar, who lives on Earth prior to the development of chemistry. When Oscar says "Water has no odor," he refers to the liquid that is H_2O. Now consider Twin-Oscar, who lives on Twin Earth prior to the development of twin-chemistry. When Twin-Oscar says "Water has no odor," it seems implausible that he is referring to the same stuff that Oscar refers to. Rather, Twin-Oscar is referring to twin-water, the liquid that is XYZ. This is so even though neither Oscar nor Twin-Oscar knows anything about the chemical makeup of water. Even so, Oscar's use of the term "water" corresponds to a different substance from Twin-Oscar's use of the word "water." People on Earth use the term "water" to refer to the kind of substance that they are in causal contact with, and people on Twin Earth use the term "water" to refer to the substance that they are in causal contact with. So Oscar's term "water" means something different from Twin-Oscar's term "water," even though from an internal perspective, they are exactly alike. Summarizing this line of reasoning, Putnam offered a simple, now-famous remark: "Meaning just ain't in the head."

In thinking about why Oscar's use of the word "water" and Twin-Oscar's use of the word "water" pick out different substances, it may help to consider an analogy to photographs. Suppose I run into Mary Kate Olsen at the airport and take a selfie with her. When you look at the photo, you might not be able to tell whether it's of Mary Kate or her identical twin Ashley. But though the photo might be indistinguishable from a photo of me with Ashely, the photo is not a photo of Ashley. Who the subject matter of the photo is – whom the photo is *of* – depends on whom the camera lens came into causal contact with. Likewise, what Oscar's word "water" means depends on which substance he is in causal contact with. The same goes for Twin-Oscar as well.

Putnam's argument concerned linguistic terms that pick out natural kinds of things in the world – not only "water," but also "gold," "tiger," "lemon," and so on. Subsequently, Tyler Burge broadened Putnam's externalism in two ways: first, by applying it to thought contents as well as linguistic contents; and second, by applying it to social kinds in addition to natural kinds (1979). For Burge, the meanings of our words are determined not just by our natural environment but by our linguistic community as well.

On the Putnam/Burge kind of externalism, our minds extend into the world by virtue of the world's determination of our meanings. For Clark and Chalmers, however, the mind extend out into the world in a much more literal way. In their view, the externalization doesn't occur by our meanings being at least partly constituted by the world outside our skull and skin, but rather by the mind itself being at least partly constituted by the world outside of our skull and skin. They thus brand their view *active externalism* to distinguish it from the more passive externalism that came before.

THE CASE OF OTTO

Clark and Chalmers published their paper on "The Extended Mind" in 1998, before cell phones were common, let alone ubiquitous. (The first flip phone was released in 1996, the first BlackBerry smartphone was released in 2003, and the iPhone premiered in 2007.) The device they use to make their case is thus rather low-tech: a simple notebook.

Consider Otto, a man in the early stages of Alzheimer's disease, who carries around a notebook with him wherever he goes. Every time he learns a new piece of information, he writes it down in his notebook. He has developed a very good system of organization, so when he needs to access a piece of information, he is able to find it in his notebook quickly and easily. For example, when he hears about a special exhibition at the Museum of Modern Art and decides to go, he consults his notebook for the location. When he finds the entry that contains the relevant information, the information that the museum is located on 53rd Street, Otto then walks to 53rd Street.

According to Clark and Chalmers, Otto's notebook functions for him analogously to the way biological memory usually functions. To see this, compare Otto to Inga, who also hears about the exhibition at the Museum of Modern Art. When she decides to go, she thinks for a moment before recalling that the Museum is located on 53rd Street. She then walks to 53rd Street. Inga had the belief that the museum is on 53rd Street even before she consulted her memory. Likewise, why shouldn't we say that Otto has the belief that the museum is on 53rd Street even before he consults his notebook? Just as Inga's process of memory consultation brings the relevant belief to her mind, Otto's process of notebook consultation brings the relevant belief to his mind.

In Chapter One, we noted the distinction between occurrent and non-occurrent mental states like beliefs. At any given moment, each of us has many, many more beliefs than the ones that are before our minds. The ones before our minds are the occurrent beliefs; the ones that are stored in memory are the non-occurrent beliefs. Non-occurrent beliefs are often also called *standing* beliefs. Those of you who have been to New York and have visited the Museum of Modern Art might share Otto and Inga's belief that it is on 53rd Street, but before you started reading this section, I suspect that this belief was not an occurrent one. Likewise, I suspect that all (or at least most) of the following claims are things you believe – that 2 + 3 = 5, that squares have four sides, that Abraham Lincoln had a beard, that Serena Williams is a tennis player. While these beliefs were presumably non-occurrent even just one minute ago, now that you have read the previous sentence they are at least momentarily occurrent. Likewise, say Clark and Chalmers, before hearing about the new exhibition at the Museum of Modern Art both Inga and Otto had non-occurrent beliefs about its location. The only difference between them arises from the fact that Inga's belief was stored in her biological mind while Otto's belief was stored in his extended mind.

THE EXTENDED MIND ARGUMENT

We can summarize the considerations put forth by Clark and Chalmers in the following argument:

The Extended Mind Argument:

1   The records in Otto's notebook play the same causal/explanatory role as non-occurrent beliefs within his brain.
2   Non-occurrent beliefs within Otto's brain are mental states of Otto's.
3   Anything that plays the same causal/explanatory role as a mental state of a subject is itself a mental state of that subject.
4   So, the records in Otto's notebook are mental states of Otto's. [From 1,2,3]
5   Anything containing some of a subject's mental states is part of that subject's mind.
6   So, the notebook is part of Otto's mind. [From 4,5]
7   So, the mind extends into the world. [From 6]

The third premise has often been referred to as the **Parity Principle**. Though the premise could be accepted by both dualists and physicalists, it is especially congenial to the functionalist approach. Given that the functionalist defines mental states in functional terms, that is, in terms of causal/explanatory roles, they should find the Parity Principle relatively unproblematic.

The premise that has probably come in for the most criticism is the first one. Even though the records in Otto's notebook prompt him to head in the direction of 53rd Street, why should we think that they really are on a par with the non-occurrent beliefs stored within his brain? Consider a case in which Inga comes across a word she's never seen before. Fortunately, she has a dictionary app on her phone, and so she looks it up. It seems wildly implausible to say that Inga has a non-occurrent belief about the meaning of the word before consulting the dictionary app.

FOUR CONDITIONS

In an attempt to forestall objections of this sort, Clark and Chalmers draw our attention to several special features concerning Otto's use of his notebook. First, though most people who use a notebook have it with them only some of the time, Otto's notebook is consistently and reliably available to him, and he calls upon it regularly. Second, whenever he does consult his notebook, he can easily retrieve the needed information. All the information is stored in such a way as to be easily accessible. Third, when Otto retrieves information from his notebook, he automatically endorses that information. Finally, any information that is present in the notebook has been consciously endorsed by Otto in the past, and that's why it has been included in the notebook. These features can be reconfigured to provide us with necessary conditions for when an external device plays the same causal/explanatory role as a non-occurrent belief:

1   The external device X is consistently and reliably available and is typically invoked;
2   The information in X is easily accessible when it is required;
3   The user of X automatically endorses information from X; and
4   The information is present in X because it was consciously endorsed by the user of X in the past.

Several of these conditions help to differentiate Otto's notebook from Inga's dictionary app. If Inga is like most of us, there are probably plenty of times that she doesn't have her phone with her, and even when she does, she probably doesn't use her dictionary app regularly. Even more so, however, the information that's included in the dictionary app was included there without her ever having even heard of it. She had never previously endorsed, or even heard of, the dictionary definition that she now accesses. Thus, it looks like the dictionary app fails to meet conditions 1 and 4.

Most of us who use notebooks or even phones probably use them much more casually and infrequently than Otto uses his notebook, and such devices are thus unlikely to meet several of Clark and Chalmers' conditions. In these cases, the information in our notebooks and phones does not function exactly like our non-occurrent beliefs, and these devices would thus not be part of our extended minds.

OBJECTIONS TO PREMISE 1

Though Clark and Chalmers' four conditions help to address some of the objections that might be brought against premise 1 of their argument, there are other objections that still pose a threat. Most such objections attempt to show that there is an important disanalogy between the records in Otto's notebook and internally stored non-occurrent beliefs. Some of these alleged disanalogies include:

a   Otto accesses the records in his notebook by perception, whereas internal beliefs are accessed by introspection;
b   Otto's notebook can be easily tampered with in a way that his internal beliefs cannot be; and
c   Otto's notebook can be shared whereas his internal beliefs cannot be.

In each case, Clark and Chalmers attempt to show that the disanalogy is not as significant as may initially appear. For example, given that both Inga and Otto have to use some means to access their stored non-occurrent beliefs, why should it matter functionally that the process of retrieval in one case goes via perception and in one case via introspection? Absent some explanation as to why this difference makes a functional difference, Clark and Chalmers can dismiss the objection as not carrying very much weight. Likewise, we have no reason to believe that internally stored beliefs cannot be tampered with. A sophisticated drug slipped into a drink might be able to wipe out a subset of one's non-occurrent memories just as easily as a pencil eraser can wipe out a subset of the records in Otto's notebook. The process of tampering will be different, but the potential for tampering remains. Finally, it's not clear that brain-based mental states are in principle unshareable. To give just one example, there is some evidence that conjoined twins Krista and Tatiana Hogan, who are fused by their skulls, share some of their sensory experiences – evidence that one twin feels pain when the other is pricked by a needle for a blood draw, or that one twin might feel a twinge below her sternum when the other slurps her juice too quickly. (We will return to this issue below in the section on Mind Mergers.)

One disanalogy that seems potentially more significant is raised by philosopher Dan Weiskopf (2008). Normally, when we learn a new piece of information, we adjust our other beliefs accordingly. These adjustments happen automatically. For example, suppose you believe that high school students Taylor and Hayden are dating, and you then also form the belief that they are going to prom together. You later hear that Taylor and Hayden have broken up, and you thus abandon your belief that they are dating. In this case, you will likely also abandon your belief that they are going to prom together. This change to your belief about their prom plans happens without any deliberation on your part. But, as Weiskopf notes, that's not how revisions to Otto's beliefs occur. When he learns that Taylor and Hayden have broken up, he'll likely erase the record "Taylor and Hayden are dating" from his notebook, or add in a "not" to what he'd previously written. But nothing else happens *automatically* to any of the other records in the notebook. Of course, Otto might mechanically search through the notebook to see if anything else needs to be changed. But this kind of deliberate, mechanical process of belief revision is entirely different from what happens with our normal non-occurrent beliefs. The problem, as Weiskopf puts it, is that Otto's notebook is not *informationally integrated* in the way that our internal occurrent beliefs are.

In response to this objection, Clark and Chalmers might simply add another condition to the four that they have previously offered. They might also require:

5   The records contained in X are informationally integrated.

Unfortunately, however, the addition of this condition prevents the Otto case from serving as an example of an extended mind.

Otto's notebook does not meet this condition, and it seems unlikely that any kind of simple tinkering to the case will enable it to meet this condition. Even the information contained in smartphones is not usually informationally integrated in this way. For example, when I enter a land line number into the contact info for one person, the contact info for their spouse is not automatically updated. Though the informational integration condition does not present an objection *in principle* to the existence of extended minds, it makes it much less likely that any such extended minds are achievable *in practice*.

OBJECTIONS TO PREMISE 2

Though premise 2 of Clark and Chalmers' argument is usually considered relatively uncontroversial, Brie Gertler has recently suggested that it should be rejected (2007). On her view, though Clark and Chalmers are right that there can be devices external to the brain that are functionally on a par with non-occurrent beliefs, this does not imply that the mind extends out into the world, because non-occurrent beliefs should not be considered part of the mind. Rather, the mind consists only of occurrent states and conscious processes.

To support this claim, Gertler reflects on our epistemic access to our own mental states. Generally speaking, the way that we each come to know about our own mental states is different from the way that we come to know about the mental states of others. To determine the mental states of others, you make an inference from their behavior. To determine your own mental states, you use introspection. You cannot introspect anyone else's mental states, nor can anyone else introspect your mental states. Introspection is, by its nature, a first-personal mode of access that one has to one's own mental states.

Earlier, in conjunction with our discussion on physicalism in Chapter Three, we noted that theorists of mind look to answer the question: what makes a mental state mental? Many philosophers - of whom Gertler is one – have invoked **introspection** to answer this question. In Gertler's view, introspectability is crucial to our basic concept of mind. What it is to be a mental state is, at least in part, to be introspectable. Since non-occurrent states are not introspectable, they are not part of the mind.

Anticipating this potential response to their argument, Clark and Chalmers reject it as "extreme." On their view, restricting the mind only to occurrent states and processes threatens to make our identities discontinuous. It's only when we accept non-occurrent states as part of the mind that we are able to see the natural connections between your mind at one moment and your mind at the next. A belief that is non-occurrent at moment t1 might become occurrent at moment t2 and then non-occurrent again at moment t3, and it can be accurately described as a belief *of yours* even when it is non-occurrent. When we deny that non-occurrent states are part of the mind, occurrent beliefs must be viewed as simply popping in and out of existence, and we have no way of attributing beliefs to you when they are not occurrent before the mind. At moments when the belief 2+3=5 is not occurrent to your mind, there isn't a real sense in which it is something you believe. On Gertler's view, though this consequence may be unpalatable, it is still better than the alternative option of giving up on introspectability.

MIND UPLOADING

If Clark and Chalmers are right that our minds can extend beyond the boundaries of skin and skull, then our increasing reliance on technological devices in the coming years may well mean that many of us offload some of our beliefs and other mental states to external storage devices. But how many such beliefs and mental states can be offloaded? Might *all* your mental states be offloaded? Or, to put the question another way, might you be able to upload your entire mind to a computer?

TECHNOLOGICAL AND PHILOSOPHICAL FEASIBILITY

In one sense, this question raises issues about our technological capabilities. Recent scientific developments suggest that these cases are not as bizarre or far-fetched as they initially appear. As far back as 2001 Kurweil argued that all of the technologies needed for mental uploading are already in existence, even though they are not yet available at the requisite speed, size, and cost (and note also that improvements in speed, size, and cost are occurring at a double exponential rate). Though the prospect of mapping a brain with enough detail to upload it to a computer may seem incredibly intimidating, Kurzweil suggests that we shouldn't be discouraged. After all, at one point the prospect of mapping the human genome also seemed incredibly intimidating, but the Human Genome Project was declared complete in 2003.

In short, while mental uploading may at present be technologically out of reach, given the technological progress that's already been made, the outcome does not seem to be an outlandish one. In a discussion of some apparently outlandish thought experiments, Derek Parfit (1984) distinguishes between the impossible and the *deeply* impossible, and we might usefully employ that distinction here: though mental uploading is presently impossible, it does not seem to be deeply impossible.

For our purposes, however, what's more interesting than whether this kind of upload would be technologically feasible is the question of whether it would be philosophically feasible. Even if we one day develop the technology necessary to upload all of our mental states to a machine, we might wonder whether futurists like Kurzweil are right to view this as a form of personal survival, perhaps even as a way to achieve immortality. In order to determine whether these potential technological developments would give us the kind of survival that we most care about, we'd need to know the answers to at least two important philosophical questions. First, would the machine with your uploaded mental states really be conscious? And even if it is, would it really be *you*?

DIFFERENT KINDS OF UPLOADING

Before we can address these questions directly, we need to think more carefully about how the uploading would proceed. Here again some recent work by David Chalmers (2010) is particularly relevant. In a paper discussing the **Singularity,** Chalmers distinguishes three different kinds of upload scenarios.

In *destructive uploading*, the scientists freeze a human brain and then analyze its structure one layer at a time. As each layer is analyzed, the distribution of neurons and other relevant components is recorded, along with all of the relevant connections between them. All of this information is then loaded to a computer, which produces a model of the original brain. Although the biological brain is destroyed through this process, if all of the analysis and transferring goes smoothly, then we might think of the computer model as a recreation of the original brain – that is, it would be plausible to describe what's occurred as a case in which the mental contents of the original biological brain are uploaded to the computer.

In *gradual uploading*, the contents of the original biological brain are slowly and steadily transferred to a computer – perhaps even neuron by neuron. Suppose, for example, that scientists were to develop nanobots, robots no bigger than the size of bloodcells, that could enter your brain and attach themselves to individual neurons. Once a nanobot gains all the information about the neuron needed in order to fully replicate its behavior, the nanobot destroys the neuron and takes its place. If the scientists do this one neuron at a time, then at the end of the process they would have created an artificial brain that is functionally equivalent to the original brain. Here again, it would be plausible to describe this as a case in which the mental contents of the original biological brain have been uploaded to a computational system.

Of course, there is no reason that the nanobots in the gradual uploading process would have to destroy the original neuron whose functions they replicate. In *nondestructive uploading*, after a nanobot gains the relevant information, it is removed and stored. Once all the needed nanobots have been programmed, they are assembled together into a computational system, perhaps by communicating with one another via high-speed wireless communication. At this point, the system they constitute is functionally equivalent to the original brain – only this time, without the original brain having been destroyed.

UPLOADING AND CONSCIOUSNESS

Suppose that, as a result of one of these uploading procedures, your mental states now reside in a computational system that we'll call *the upload*. The first philosophically important question to ask about the upload is whether it has consciousness. How one answers this question will to a large extent depend on one's theory of the mind. Let's first think about the dualist view. It looks like the theory should be compatible with the upload being conscious, but we don't get much guidance on how to make this determination. The theory itself doesn't tell us which kinds of material entities have conscious minds. Turning next to physicalism, it seems pretty clear that on most varieties of the view, the answer will be no. Since most physicalists take consciousness to be a biological phenomenon, the fact that the upload does not have a biological brain precludes it from being conscious. Finally, turning to functionalism, it seems pretty clear that the answer will be yes. Given that the upload has the same functional organization as the human brain, and given that human brains are conscious, the upload too should be conscious.

Let's focus for a moment on an upload that has been produced via a process of gradual uploading. Indeed, it's this kind of process that futurists like Kurzweil see as the most likely way that we'll transition from fully biological beings to at least partly non-biological ones. The gradual uploading process might be completed in a matter of minutes or, more likely, it might take place much more slowly over the course of several years. Before the process begins, the human being whose mental states are about to be uploaded was a conscious being. There are, says Chalmers, three possibilities for what happens to that consciousness during the process of uploading. First, it might suddenly disappear at some point in the process. Second, it might gradually fade out over time. Or third, it might stay present throughout. Chalmers suggests that the third possibility is the most plausible.

The first possibility, sudden disappearance, is particularly implausible. We can see this most clearly by focusing on the issue of timing, that is, by asking when exactly the consciousness allegedly disappears. Surely it doesn't happen after the very first neuron is replaced by a nanobot. Surely it also doesn't happen after the very last neuron is replaced by a nanobot. The subtraction of a single neuron hardly seems to be the kind of thing that could instantly and completely turn the lights out completely, consciousness-wise. Once we recognize this point, we can see why there's no plausible moment in the process where consciousness would just switch completely off.

Initially, the possibility of a gradually fading consciousness seems considerably more plausible. On closer examination, however, this

possibility too proves problematic. One problem is that of con-
ceptualizing exactly what the hypothesis means. Would visual
experience become gradually washed out and less vivid, perhaps
fading to black and white before disappearing entirely? Or
would we lose one modality of sensory experience at a time,
with our sense of smell fading first, and then our sense of
hearing, and then our sense of sight, and so on? But even if we
could pin down what it means for consciousness to fade gradually, there is a further, deeper issue. The problem, as Chalmers notes, is that the upload is, by hypothesis, functionally
identical to the original human throughout the entire process.
This means that there is no noticeable change either internally,
to the human/upload themselves, or externally, to other people.
As Chalmers notes, if the fading consciousness view were correct, a human being who has been partially uploaded "will be
wandering around with a highly degraded consciousness,
although they will be functioning as always and swearing that
nothing has changed." Thus, the fading consciousness proposal
seems as unworkable as the sudden disappearance proposal. As
Chalmers concludes, the hypothesis that consciousness will stay
fully present throughout the uploading process is "by far the
most plausible" of the three possibilities.

UPLOADING AND PERSONAL IDENTITY

The issue of personal identity over time – of what makes a person
at one time identical to a person at some other time – is a complicated one, and we cannot hope to tackle it in any great detail
here. In ordinary cases of survival through time, we have both
bodily continuity and mental continuity. Puzzle cases arise when
these two kinds of continuity come apart. One standard puzzle
case involves a scenario in which two individuals seem to have
swapped bodies. Here think of the kind of thing that happens in
the 2003 movie *Freaky Friday*, when teenager Anna Coleman
(played by Lindsay Lohan) and her mother Tess (played by Jamie
Lee Curtis) wake up one day to discover that something very
strange has happened: all of Tess's thoughts and memories seem
now to be "housed" in Anna's body, while all of Anna's thoughts
and memories seem now to be "housed" in Tess's body.

Confronted with this kind of case, many people are inclined to think that Tess now exists in Anna's former body while Anna now exists in Tess's former body. In other words, when it comes to personal identity, body swap cases suggest that mental continuity trumps bodily continuity. But there are other kinds of cases that suggest the opposite conclusion. For example, when someone suffers from significant amnesia, we typically don't take the lack of mental continuity to mean that the previous person no longer exists.

Upload cases often seem to strike people like body swap cases. Just as Anna might house her thoughts and memories in her mom's body, she might also house her thoughts and memories in a machine. But here a significant wrinkle appears. In cases of destructive uploading, it might seem plausible to think that the machine system that now contains Anna's thoughts and memories is Anna. But what about in cases of non-destructive uploading? At the end of such procedures, not only are we presented with a machine system that houses all of Anna's thoughts and memories but we also are presented with Anna herself, who remains unharmed by the uploading procedure. Even worse, there's no reason that we couldn't repeat the nondestructive uploading process, or perform it many times at once, such that there might be five or even five thousand machine systems all of which house Anna's thoughts and memories. They can't *all* be Anna. In discussions of personal identity, this worry is often referred to as the *problem of reduplication.*

But let's keep things simpler and just focus on a nondestructive uploading case where there is only a single upload. Before the procedure, we have Anna (call her *AnnaB*, for before). After the procedure we have Anna (*AnnaA*, for after) and the machine system with her uploaded consciousness (*Upload*). It seems pretty plausible that AnnaA is the same person as AnnaB. The only thing that's happened in between is an entirely non-destructive process. It also seems clear that AnnaA and Upload are distinct entities. They are in different places at the same time, they are having different experiences, and so on. But that means that Upload cannot be the same person as AnnaB. If they were, we'd have a violation of the simple principle of transitivity of identity. According to this principle, if a is identical to b, and b is identical to c, then a is identical to c. In this case, if Upload were identical to AnnaB, then given that AnnaB is identical to AnnaA, Upload would have to be identical to AnnaA.

But since Upload has the same kind of relationship with AnnaB – a relationship of full mental continuity – as the relationship that an upload would have to Anna in a destructive uploading case, we now have reason to question whether the upload in the destructive case is really Anna. We can put this argument in standard form as follows:

The Argument for Pessimism about Uploading:

1 The upload in the destructive case has the same relationship of mental continuity to Anna as the upload in the non-destructive case.
2 If the upload is not identical to Anna in the non-destructive case, then the upload is not identical to Anna in the destructive case.
3 The upload is not identical to Anna in the non-destructive case.
4 Thus, the upload is not identical to Anna in the destructive case.

This kind of pessimistic argument has some weight. But there is also a weighty argument that can be offered in support of a more optimistic conclusion about uploading. Such an argument works somewhat analogously to the argument we considered about consciousness and uploading. There we noted that it seems unlikely that the destruction of a single neuron could wipe out consciousness. Likewise, we might think that it seems unlikely that the destruction of a single neuron could wipe out personal identity. Just as the subtraction of a single neuron hardly seems to be the kind of thing that could instantly and completely turn the lights out, consciousness-wise, it seems unlikely that the subtraction of a single neuron could instantly and completely eradicate one's personal identity. As before, once we take note of this point, we can see why there's no plausible moment in a process of gradual destructive uploading where one's personal identity would be eradicated. Having considered both the case for pessimism and the case for optimism, Chalmers himself is inclined to think that we should be optimistic. In his view, "if at some point in the future I am faced with the choice between uploading and continuing in an increasingly slow biological embodiment, then as long as I have the option of gradual uploading, I will be happy to do so."

MIND MERGERS

"I was born human. But this was an accident of fate – a condition merely of time and place. I believe it's something we have the power to change." So wrote British researcher Kevin Warwick, the self-proclaimed World's First Cyborg, in a 2000 article in *Wired*. In 1988, Warwick underwent a surgical procedure that installed a silicon chip transponder in his forearm. Following the surgery, this chip emitted a signal that enabled Warwick to directly operate the doors, lights, heaters, and computers in the Department of Cybernetics at the University of Reading. In 2002, Warwick underwent a second procedure that implanted a 4mm x 4mm electrode array into the median nerve fibers of his left arm. Following this surgery, Warwick was able to transmit neural signals directly from his peripheral nervous system to a computer.

One more surgery was yet to come, only this one was not on Warwick himself but on his wife. As he wrote:

> We'd like to send movement and emotion signals from one person to the other, possibly via the Internet. My wife, Irena, has bravely volunteered to go ahead with his-and-hers implants. The way she puts it is that if anyone is going to jack into my limbic system – to know definitively when I'm feeling happy, depressed, angry, or even sexually aroused – she wants it to be her.
>
> Irena and I will investigate the whole range of emotion and sensation. If I move a hand or finger, then send those signals to Irena, will she make the same movement? I think it likely she'll feel something. Might she feel the same pain as I do? If I sprained my ankle, could I send the signal to Irena to make her feel as though she has injured herself?

In tests following Irena's surgery, they accomplished their goal of establishing a direct link-up between their two nervous systems. The couple were able to send signals to one another back and forth through their implants. For example, when Irena would tap her finger three times, Kevin would himself feel three pulses. They were able to perceive these transmitted signals with over 98 percent accuracy.

THE FUTURE OF THE MIND   143

The connection between the Warwicks was an extremely minimal one, but it serves as a primitive first step towards what we might describe as telepathic communication. Would it be possible to achieve an even tighter connection between minds, something akin to the Vulcan mind meld on *Star Trek*? (When a Vulcan does a mind meld with another organism, they are able temporarily to merge their own mind with the mind of another and thereby feel what the other is feeling.) Just as we might be able to use technology to extend the mind or to upload the mind, might we also be able to use technology to merge our minds with others?

A REAL-LIFE CASE?

Above we briefly considered the case of conjoined twins Krista and Tatiana Hogan, who are fused at the skull. Craniopagus twins are extremely rare, occurring only once in every 2.5 million births; most such twins die within twenty-four hours of birth. The specific way that the Hogan twins' brains are connected to one another makes them unique even among craniopagus twins. The connection occurs via a neural bridge that directly links their two thalmuses. The thalmus, a mass of gray matter in the diencephalon, a part of the forebrain, is generally thought to have several key functions. It relays sensory signals and motor signals and plays a role in the regulation of both sleep and consciousness.

In an effort to give their children as normal an upbringing as possible given the circumstances, the Hogans' parents have not allowed researchers much access to the girls. The only studies they have permitted are ones that are medically necessary. But in day-to-day interactions, the girls reveal an incredible amount of mental interconnectedness. As we noted above, there is evidence that the girls share some of their sensory experiences. One twin can feel pain when the other is pricked by a needle for a blood draw, and one twin can feel a twinge below her sternum when the other slurps her juice too quickly. When they were babies, putting a pacifier in one twin's mouth could stop the other twin from crying. In a documentary taped when the girls were ten years old, their mother Felicia Simms holds an object in front of Tatiana's eyes while Krista's eyes are closed, and Krista then reports various facts about the object: what kind of toy animal it is, what its color is, and so on. The documentary also shows the same happening in reverse when an object is held in front of Krista's eyes while Tatiana's are closed. In another scene, their mother touches each twin on the leg or arm or face while the other twin's eyes are closed, and in each case, the twin with closed eyes can report where her sister was being touched.

THE UNITY OF CONSCIOUSNESS

There are many instances in ordinary life when we can intuit the experiences of others. An empathetic spouse might be able to tell with a high degree of accuracy what their spouse is feeling. But no matter how empathetic a person is, they do not literally share the feeling of the other person. Their knowledge of the other person's states comes from intuition or inference, not from **introspection**. In this way, the case of the Hogan twins seems importantly different. Normally, a person has introspective access only to their own mental states. But each Hogan twin can introspectively access some of the mental states of the other Hogan twin. This is why the case seems so persuasively to be one of mind merger (or at least partial mind merger).

Thinking about the possibility of mind merger raises questions about the unity of consciousness. We briefly encountered the suggestion that consciousness is unified when we considered Descartes' Argument from Divisibility back in Chapter Two. But while it's contentious whether considerations of unity can be used to support a dualistic theory of mind, much less contentious is the claim that an individual's conscious experiences are unified. Suppose you're walking home. You feel a gust of wind on your face, see a passing car, and hear a squeal as it takes a curve too quickly. Your bodily sensation, visual experience, and auditory experience are all taken in together as aspects of a single conscious experience. This seems to hold for all conscious subjects and all conscious experiences: if at any time someone is experiencing both A and B, these experiences are not truly separate but are experienced as A-and-B-together.

In ordinary cases, the point we just made is a transitive one. If A and B are experienced together at some time, and B and C are experienced together at some time, then A and C are experienced ogether at that time. What's striking about the Hogan case is that transitivity fails. Since the neural link between the Hogans does not seem to allow them to share all their experiences, one twin might experience A and B together at a certain time (perhaps Tatiana has an itch on her right toe while she shares Krista's visual experience) and the other twin might experience B and C together at that same time (perhaps Krista has an itch on her left toe while Tatiana is sharing her visual experience), but no one experiences A and C together at that time (because neither of the girls can feel the other's itch). The failure of transitivity occurs because the mind sharing between the twins is a partial one. The same holds true for the mind sharing between Kevin and Irena Warwick. In any complete case of mind merger, it seems that we would have to have complete unity of consciousness.

THE CONCEPTUAL POSSIBILITY OF MIND MERGERS

Would a complete mind merger be possible? Our discussion thus far suggests that there is no reason to think it is conceptually incoherent. After all, given the actual existence of partial mergers, it looks like we can just conceptually extend the case, in the way that we can conceive of perfect vacuums based on what we know about partial vacuums. That said, there are several conceptual questions that do seem to arise when we think more carefully about the matter. For example, when two individual minds are merged, is there a way to distinguish whose experience is whose? Suppose the Warwicks were able to achieve a complete mind merger, and suppose they each at their respective offices. When a car horn blares outside Kevin's office window, and they both experience the auditory sensation, does it feel to Irena like it's her own auditory sensation? Or can she tell that it's "really" Kevin's, that is, that the experience originated because of sound waves travelling into his ear canal? Relatedly, do their experiences themselves merge or do they stay distinct? Suppose that when they both simultaneously try a bite of the chef's special at their local café, Irena finds it delicious and Kevin finds it disgusting. Do they each experience simultaneous and separate deliciousness and disgust experiences, or do they each have a conjoint delicious-and-disgusting experience?

There are some difficult issues here to puzzle over. We are helped in thinking about some of them by considering a distinction drawn by Uriah Kriegel (2009) between two different aspects of phenomenal consciousness: the *qualitative* aspect and the *subjective* aspect. When I look at a red apple, there is something that it is like for me to have that visual experience; in particular, there is a reddish way it is like for me to have that visual experience. The qualitative aspect consists in the reddishness, while the subjective aspect consists in the way in which the experience is *for me*, or what we might think of as its *for-me-ness*.

In the case of a mind merger, perhaps the for-me-ness of an experience, its subjective aspect, differs depending on where the experience originates. A sound that originates via sound waves in Kevin's ear canal might have a different for-me-ness for Irena than a sound that originates in her own ear canal. Likewise for the experience of disgust originating from Kevin's bite of the chef's special, which might have a different for-me-ness for Irena than the experience of deliciousness that originated from her own bite.

THE TECHNOLOGICAL POSSIBILITY OF MIND MERGERS

But even if complete mergers are conceptually possible, are they technologically possible? In an article in *Scientific American* (Begley 2011), neuroscientist Miguel A.L. Nicolelis describes his work with the Walk Again Project, a group that aims to use brain-machine interfaces to restore complete mobility to patients with severe cases of paralysis. Nicolelis predicts that the development of this kind of technology will unlock the potential for all kinds of direct interaction between the human brain and computational devices. From there, it's only a short step to our complete liberation from the brain. And once that happens, human minds could link together in conscious network, what he calls a "collectively thinking brain-net."

Nicolelis's reasoning suggests that there is a tight link between mind-uploading and mind-merger technology. What he describes in terms of liberation from the brain is essentially the scenario we considered above in our discussion of uploading – be it gradual or destructive. Thus, insofar as we have reason to believe that mind uploading is technologically possible, it looks like we have reason to believe that mind merging is technologically possible as well.

As our discussion thus far undoubtedly suggests, normally there seems to be a one-to-one correlation between persons and streams of consciousness: one person to one stream of consciousness. Complete mind mergers, if they were possible, would present us with cases in which we had two people to one stream of consciousness. Interestingly, there are some real-life phenomena that seem to present us with a different violation of this normal correlation. In particular, there are some phenomena in which we seem to have one person to two (or more) streams of consciousness.

We briefly encountered one such phenomenon in Chapter Two: dissociative identity disorder. Recall that an individual with DID seems to have two or more distinct personality states, typically called alters. The alters tend to have executive control of the body at different times, and an alter often doesn't have any memories of what's happened when they are not in charge of the body. When the alters have entirely distinct streams of consciousness from one another, we might seem to have a case in which there is more than one stream of consciousness to a single person.

Another such phenomenon occurs in cases in which an individual has undergone a **hemispherectomy**, a surgical procedure in which the two hemispheres of the brain are disconnected from one another by the severing of the corpus callosum. The surgery, which is rare, is usually performed as a treatment for severe epilepsy or other seizure disorders. By severing the connection between the two hemispheres, doctors believe they can reduce the impact of seizures by preventing them from spreading from one hemisphere to the other hemisphere. In ordinary life post-surgery, patients do not seem to exhibit any signs that their brains have been cut. However, in certain situations, particularly in controlled experimental environments, the patients behave in such a way that suggests there is a breakdown in the unity of consciousness.

For the most part, the left hemisphere of the brain has control over the right side of the body and the right hemisphere has control over the left side of the body. Through various experimental techniques, researchers working with hemispherectomy patients were able to send visual signals only to one side of the brain. Since the left hemisphere generally has control of language, if information was presented only to the right hemisphere, the patient could not verbally report on it. So, for example, if the researchers flashed the word "hat" only to the right hemisphere, the patient would deny that they saw anything. However, if a group of objects were accessible to them, they would pick out the hat with their left hand (controlled by the right hemisphere). The hemispheres thus appear to be in conflict with one another. Further experiments generated additional evidence of both conflicts and the independent operation of the hemispheres. One patient, for example, could easily draw a square with one hand while simultaneously drawing a circle with his other hand – something that people whose hemispheres are connected have difficulty doing.

Here again, as was the case with DID, we might think that there are two streams of consciousness associated with a single person. Certainly this is what many researchers working with these patients have concluded. As Roger Sperry, one of the leading researchers in the field, put it: "Instead of the normally unified stream of consciousness, these patients behave in many ways as if they have two independent streams of conscious awareness, each of which is cut off from and out of contact with the mental experiences of the other" (1968, 724).

But because hemispherectomy patients typically do not reveal any disunity in ordinary life, how exactly to assess the situation is a complicated issue. At the very least, however, even if there aren't two disconnected streams of consciousness, there does seem to be some kind of breakdown in the normal unity of consciousness, where every conscious experience that we attribute to an individual at a particular time is co-conscious with every other conscious experience that the individual has at that time.

It's also interesting to reflect on whether hemispherectomy results shed any light on the debate between dualism and physicalism. On the one hand, if we focus on the integration of the patient's mind in most all circumstances, we might reason like this: insofar as the complete separation of the brain does not yield two separate minds, the phenomenon counts in favor of the dualist. On the other hand, if we focus on the division in the patient's mind in the experimental circumstances, we might deny that there is still a single mind there. We might then reason like this: given that splitting the brain in two also splits the mind in two, the phenomenon counts in favor of the physicalist.

Of course, there are responses each theorist could make to the reasoning that their opponent offers. The dualist might stress that it is fully compatible with their theory that changes to the brain will result in changes to the mind. This result does not require identity between the two but could also be explained by a causal relationship between the two. But the physicalist might also make an additional point: trying to accommodate the experimental data from the hemispherectomy patients suggests that we might not have as clear a handle on what counts as a mind as we might have thought.

CONCLUDING REMARKS

In this final chapter, we considered three different ways that technology may impact the mind. From mind extension to mind uploading to mind merging, we have seen ways that the future of the human mind may be significantly different from its past. As we have seen, though matters are far from fully settled, there is reason to think that each of these scenarios is not only conceptually possible but technologically possible as well.

Though the discussion here has been a bit more speculative than the discussion in the previous five chapters, often veering into territory that is typically the domain of science fiction, it's here useful to recall our discussion of the method of thought experimentation from all the way back in Chapter One. By engaging with **thought experiments**, we are often able to reveal important aspects of the concepts with which we are working. In this case, the scenarios considered here help us to unpack more fully the very notion of mind with which we've been operating throughout the entire book.

FURTHER READING

There are many useful papers discussing the extended mind thesis in Menary (2010), including a further discussion by Clark drawing on *Memento*, a 2000 film directed by Christopher Nolan that presents a compelling example of an extended mind at work. Clark (2003) presents an accessible discussion of the extended mind thesis and even extends that thesis further.

The discussion in this chapter of mind uploading raises many issues concerning personal identity. For an introduction to this topic, see Kind (2015), especially

Chapters Two to Four. Criticisms of Chalmers' optimistic approach to uploading can be found in Corabi and Schneider (2014) and Pigliucci (2014).

Kevin Warwick describes the cybernetic procedures he underwent in Warwick (2004). The Hogan twins are chronicled in the documentary *Inseparable*, though at this time, the film is available for viewing only in Canada. Excerpts are available at https://www.cbc.ca/cbcdocspov/ep isodes/inseparable. Further information about the Hogans is available in the *New York Times* article "Could Conjoined Twins Share a Mind?" available at https://www.nytimes.com/2011/05/29/magazine/could-con joined-twins-share-a-mind.html.

As noted in this chapter, examples of mind mergers and collective consciousness are rife in science fiction. Demonstrations of the Vulcan mind meld are found in "Dagger of the Mind" and "The Devil in the Dark," episodes of *Star Trek: The Original Series*. A famous example of collective consciousness comes from the example of the Borg, a cyborg species that appears in *Star Trek: The Next Generation*; see, for example, the episodes "Q Who?" and "The Best of Both Worlds," as well as the 1996 movie *Star Trek: First Contact*. For another example of mind merger in science fiction, see the story "Soul Mate" (Sutton 1959). The first discussion of the philosophical implications regarding hemispherectomy patients came in Nagel (1971), and the paper raised many issues that continue to be discussed today. A video exploration of the phenomenon, "Severed Corpus Callosum," is available at https://www.youtube.com/watch?v=82tlVcq6E7A& feature=youtu.be. The video, produced by *Scientific American Frontiers*, is narrated by actor Alan Alda.

Schneider and Mandik (2018) discuss various emerging technologies – including many of those that we have discussed in this chapter – and offer some speculations on the challenges they will bring. In their view, philosophy of mind is well poised to help society navigate these challenges.

GLOSSARY

A posteriori   When a statement cannot be known **a priori** but can only be known a posteriori, this knowledge depends in some way on experience or observation. For example, one cannot know that it is raining outside or that it was raining yesterday without relying in some way on experience (including memories of past experiences).

A priori   When a statement can be known a priori, it is known independent of experience or observation. For example, one can know that squares have four sides, or that bachelors are unmarried, simply by virtue of understanding the notion of squares and bachelors respectively, even if one has never had any experience of squares or of bachelors. The notion of the a priori typically contrasts with the **a posteriori**.

Anti-nesting principle   A principle often invoked in discussions of consciousness that claims that consciousness cannot "nest," that is, that any conscious entity cannot be composed of any parts that are themselves conscious.

Argument   A piece of logical reasoning containing a claim or set of claims offered to support some further claim. The claim being supported is called the **conclusion**, while the reasons offered in support of it are called **premises**.

Behaviorism   A **physicalist** theory popular in the early 20th century that attempted to reduce mind to behavior. On the behaviorist view, all that it is to be in a particular mental state is to be disposed to behave in certain characteristic ways.

Bodily Response Theory   A theory of emotion that claims that emotion consists in the recognition of the collection of bodily

responses (such as changes in heart rate, blood pressure, hor
monal releases, and so on) that result from certain situations
Each emotion is characterized by a different set of such bodil
responses. The bodily response theory is often contrasted wit
the **judgment theory**.

Conclusion   The final claim of an **argument** and the one tha
the other claims are put forth to support. The other claims i
the argument are called **premises**.

Deductive Argument   An **argument** in which the **premises** ar
put forth in an effort to guarantee the truth of the **conclusion**.

Direction of fit   A property of propositional attitudes that cap
tures whether they aim to have their content match the worl
(mind-to-world direction of fit) or whether they aim to mak
the world match their content (world-to-mind direction of fit`

Dualism   The theory of mind that claims that there are tw
fundamentally different kinds of things in the world, those tha
are physical and those that are mental. Dualism is usuall
contrasted with **monism**, and more specifically, with **phy
sicalism**. It comes in two main versions, **substance dualism**
and **property dualism**.

Eliminative Materialism   A version of **physicalism** that denie
that mental states can be reduced to physical states and claim
instead that mental states should be eliminated from our ontology

Epiphenomenalism   A **dualist** account of mental causation tha
claims that the mental has no causal efficacy with respect to th
physical. While the epiphenomenalist typically accepts that phy
sical events can cause mental events, they deny that mental even
can cause physical events. Though it may seem to me that m
desire for a cookie causes me to get up, that is merely an illusior
Epiphenomenalists are usually **property dualists** rather tha
substance dualists, and their view usually contrasts wit
interactionism.

Epistemology   The subfield of philosophy that aims to investi
gate questions concerning knowledge, belief, and justificatior
Epistemology is often contrasted with **metaphysics**.

Experimental Philosophy   An approach to philosophy tha
incorporates the experimental methods of psychology and cog
nitive science in an attempt to address traditional philosophic.
questions, usually by way of the study of intuitions. Experiment.

philosophy is a relatively new development, having only really emerged in the early 21st century.

Externalism   A view that claims that what an individual means by a certain word does not depend solely on the state of the subject but also depends upon the external environment the subject is in. This view, especially as extended not just to words but also to the content of thoughts, is also often called anti-individualism.

Functionalism   A theory of mind that claims that mental states should be understood in functional terms. For the functionalist, a mental state is the state that it is because of its function, not because of its constitution.

Hard Problem of Consciousness   The problem of explaining why and how phenomenal experience arises from the physical processing of the brain. The hard problem contrasts with other easier (though by no means easy) problems about consciousness that explore psychological processing and functional mechanisms.

Hemispherectomy   A surgical procedure in which the corpus callosum, the thick band of nerve fibers connecting the two hemispheres of the brain, is cut.

Idealism   A version of **monism** that claims that everything that exists is immaterial/nonphysical. Idealism is usually contrasted with **materialism/physicalism**.

Identity Theory   A version of physicalism that claims that mental states are identical to brain states.

Inductive Argument   An **argument** in which the **premises** are put forth in an effort to make the truth of the **conclusion** more probable.

Intentionality   The aspect of our mental states by virtue of which they are about events or things or states of affairs, i.e., by virtue of which they are representational. In this sense, intentionality has nothing to do with our intentions; it is completely independent of whether a state is deliberately or voluntarily formed.

Interactionism   A **dualist** account of mental causation that claims that there is two-way causal interaction between the mental and the physical: mental events cause physical events, as when my desire for a cookie prompts me to stand up, and physical events cause mental events, as when the contact between my foot and a sharp tack causes me to feel pain. Interactionism contrasts with **epiphenomenalism**.

Introspection   The process by which we come to have direct and distinctly first-personal knowledge of our own mental states.

Judgment Theory   A theory of emotion that claims that emotions consist in certain kinds of judgments or appraisals of the world. Unlike the **bodily response theory**, with which it is usually contrasted, the judgment theory treats emotions as fundamentally cognitive in nature.

Leibniz' Law   A philosophical principle, named after the German philosopher Gottfried Leibniz, that claims the following: if two things A and B are identical to one another, then they share all their properties in common.

Logic   The subfield of philosophy that aims to explore the structure and nature of reasoning. A significant part of logic consists in the evaluation of **arguments**.

Materialism   A theory of mind that claims that everything that exists is made of matter. Contemporary versions of materialism are generally referred to as **physicalist** views.

Metaphysics   The subfield of philosophy that explores the structure and nature of reality. Metaphysics is often contrasted with **epistemology**.

Monism   The view that there is one fundamental kind of thing in the world. Monists divide primarily into two categories: **idealists**, who believe that everything that exists is immaterial/nonphysical, and **materialists** (also called **physicalists**) who believe that everything that exists is material/physical. A third kind of monism, **Russellian monism**, claims that the one fundamental kind of thing cannot be described in the terms of either traditional idealism or traditional materialism.

Multiple Realizability   The claim that a given property or kind of thing can be realized in many different kinds of physical substrates. With respect to the mind, the claim is that mental states can be realized in many different kinds of physical substrates. Multiple realizability of the mental is often thought to count against the **identity theory** and in favor of **functionalism**.

Necessary Condition   When some fact or state of affairs A is a necessary condition for some other fact or state of affairs B, B will not obtain unless A obtains (though A may obtain without B obtaining). Necessary conditions are often contrasted with **sufficient conditions**.

Ockham's Razor (also Occam's Razor)   A principle associated with medieval philosopher William of Ockham that states that entities should not be posited beyond necessity. More generally, Ockham's Razor connects with principles of simplicity that suggest that, other things being equal, the simpler theory should be preferred.

Physicalism   A theory of mind that claims that everything that exists is physical and thus that the mind is nothing over and above the physical. Physicalism is often characterized in terms of **supervenience**, i.e., the claim that the mental supervenes on the physical. Physicalism, which used to be referred to as **materialism**, comes in several varieties, including the **identity theory** and **eliminative materialism**.

Premise   One of a set of claims put forth in support of a further claim, called the **conclusion**. The premises and conclusion together make up an **argument**.

Property Dualism   A version of **dualism**. Property dualists think that the only kinds of substances that exist are physical ones, but they think that at least some substances have mental properties in addition to their physical properties. Property dualism is usually contrasted with **substance dualism**.

Propositional Attitudes   The mental states that consist in taking an attitude or a stance toward a particular content. Paradigmatic examples of propositional attitudes are beliefs and desires. When we believe a content like *tomorrow it will be sunny* we take a different attitude towards the content from what we do when we desire that same content. Propositional attitudes are all states with **intentionality**.

Qualia   The qualitative properties of experiences. What it feels like, experientially, to see a red heart emoji is different from what it feels like to see a purple heart emoji. The qualia of these experiences are what give each of them its characteristic "feel" and what distinguish them from one another.

Russellian Monism   A monist view that attempts to strike a balance between traditional dualist views and traditional physicalist views. In this view, there exist fundamental properties that ground all structural and relational things.

The Singularity   The point in our technological development at which machine intelligence will exceed human intelligence.

Soundness   A property of good **deductive arguments**. When a deductive argument is sound, it is both **valid** and has true **premises**. This means that the **conclusion** of a sound argument is always true.

Substance Dualism   A version of **dualism**. Substance dualists think that there are two fundamentally different kinds of substances in the world, mental substances and physical substances. Substance dualism is usually contrasted with **property dualism**.

Sufficient Condition   When some fact or state of affairs A is a sufficient condition for some other fact or state of affairs B, the obtaining of A will guarantee the obtaining of B. Importantly, B may obtain without A obtaining, but if A obtains, B must obtain. Sufficient conditions are often contrasted with **necessary conditions**.

Supervenience   When some fact A supervenes on some fact or set of facts B, there cannot be a difference with respect to A unless there is a difference with respect to B. **Physicalists** typically claim that the mental supervenes on the physical, that is, that there can be no difference with respect to the mental facts of two beings unless there is a difference with respect to the physical facts of those beings.

Synesthesia   A condition in which (a) an experience in one sensory modality automatically triggers an experience in a different sensory modality (as when someone "tastes shapes") or (b) an experience with one kind of sensory feature automatically triggers an experience of a different sensory feature (as when someone sees numbers as colored).

Thought Experiments   A method used in philosophy to explore hypothetical scenarios. Typically, the imagined scenario sheds light on the coherence of a theory or its implications.

Token Physicalism   A species of **physicalism** that claims that every token mental event is identical to or consists in some token physical event. Token physicalism usually contrasts with **type physicalism**.

Type Physicalism   A species of physicalism that claims that every mental state type can be identified with a physical state type. Type physicalism usually contrasts with **token physicalism**.

Validity   A property of good **deductive arguments**. When a deductive argument is valid, the truth of the **premises** guarantees the truth of the **conclusion**.

Zombie   A creature who is physically and behaviorally indistinguishable from a human being but who is completely devoid of phenomenal consciousness.

BIBLIOGRAPHY

Alter, Torin & Nagasawa, Yujin (eds.) (2015). *Consciousness in the Physic World: Perspectives on Russellian Monism*. Oxford: Oxford University Press.

Alter, Torin & Walter, Sven (eds.) (2007). *Phenomenal Concepts and Phenomen Knowledge. New Essays on Consciousness and Physicalism*. Oxford: Oxfor University Press.

Andrews, Kristin (2015). *The Animal Mind*. Abingdon, Oxon: Routledge.

Baker, Alan (2016). "Simplicity." *The Stanford Encyclopedia of Philosophy* (Winte Edward N. Zalta (ed.). Available at: https://plato.stanford.edu/archives win2016/entries/simplicity/.

Bayne, Tim & Spener, Maja (2010). "Introspective humility." *Philosophic Issues* 20 (1): 1–22.

Begley, Sharon (2011). "Texture Messaging: Breakthrough May Help Spin Cord Patients Experience Tactile Sensations." *Scientific American*, October Available at: https://www.scientificamerican.com/article/breakthrough-may help-spinal-cord-patients-experience-tactie-sensations/.

Beha, Christopher (2017). "Headscratcher: Can Neuroscience Finally Expla Consciousness." *Harper's Magazine* (May): 88–94.

Bisson, Terry (1991). "Meat." *Omni* (April). Available at: https://web.archive org/web/20190501130711/http://www.terrybisson.com/theyre-made-out-of-meat-2/.

Block, Ned (1978). "Troubles with functionalism." *Minnesota Studies in t Philosophy of Science* 9: 261–325.

Boden, Margaret (ed.) (1990) *The Philosophy of Artificial Intelligence*. New Yor Oxford University Press.

Brentano, Franz (1874). *Psychology From an Empirical Standpoint*. Abingdo Routledge.

Brook, Andrew & Stainton, Robert J. (2000). *Knowledge and Mind: A Phil sophical Introduction*. Cambridge MA: MIT Press/A Bradford Books.

Burge, Tyler (1979). "Individualism and the mental." *Midwest Studies in Philosophy* 4 (1): 73–122.

Chalmers, David J. (1995). "The puzzle of conscious experience." *Scientific American* 273 (6): 80–86.

Chalmers, David J. (1996). *The Conscious Mind: In Search of a Fundamental Theory*. New York: Oxford University Press USA.

Chalmers, David J. (2010). "The singularity: A philosophical analysis." *Journal of Consciousness Studies* 17 (9–10): 7–65.

Chiang, Ted (2002). *Stories of Your Life and Others*. New York: Tor Press.

Churchland, Patricia (1986). *Neurophilosophy: Toward a Unified Science of the Mind/Brain*. Cambridge, MA: MIT Press.

Churchland, Paul (1981). "Eliminative materialism and the propositional attitudes." *Journal of Philosophy* 78: 67–90.

Churchland, Paul (1985). "Reduction, qualia, and the direct introspection of brain states." *Journal of Philosophy* 82: 8–28.

Churchland, Paul (1988). *Matter and Consciousness*, revised edition. Cambridge, MA: MIT Press.

Churchland, Paul (1989). "Knowing qualia. A reply to Jackson." in *A Neurocomputational Perspective: The Nature of Mind and the Structure of Science*. Cambridge, MA: MIT Press, pp. 67–76.

Clark, Andy & Chalmers, David J. (1998). "The extended mind." *Analysis* 58 (1): 7–19.

Clark, Andy (2003). *Natural-Born Cyborgs: Minds, Technologies, and the Future of Human Intelligence*. New York: Oxford University Press.

Conee, Earl (1985). "Physicalism and phenomenal qualities." *Philosophical Quarterly* 35 (July): 296–302.

Corabi, Joseph & Schneider, Susan (2014). "If you upload, will you survive?" In Russell Blackford and Damien Broderick, *Intelligence Unbound: The Future of Uploaded and Machine Minds*. Malden, MA: John Wiley and Sons, pp.131–145.

Cytowic, Richard (1993). *The Man Who Tasted Shapes*. New York: Putnam.

Damasio, Antonio R. (1994). *Descartes' Error: Emotion, Reason, and the Human Brain*. New York: G.P. Putnam's Sons.

Davidson, Donald (1982). "Rational Animals." *Dialectica*, 36: 317–328.

Deigh, John (2009). "Concepts of emotion in modern philosophy and psychology." In Peter Goldie (ed.), *The Oxford Handbook of Philosophy of Emotion*. Oxford: Oxford University Press.

Dennett, Daniel C. (1988). "Quining qualia." In Anthony J. Marcel & E. Bisiach (eds.), *Consciousness and Contemporary Science*. Oxford: Oxford University Press.

Dennett, Daniel C. (1991). *Consciousness Explained*. Boston: Little, Brown, & Co.

Dennett, Daniel C. (1995). "The unimagined preposterousness of zombies." *Journal of Consciousness Studies* 2 (4): 322–326.

Deroy, Ophelia (ed.) (2017). *Sensory Blending: On Synaesthesia and Related Phenomena*. Oxford:Oxford University Press.

Descartes, René (1641/1986). *Meditations on First Philosophy: With Selections From the Objections and Replies*. Translated by John Cottingham. Cambridge: Cambridge University Press.

Dneprov, Anatoly (1961). "The Game." *Knowledge is Power* 5: 39–42. Available at: http://www.hardproblem.ru/en/posts/Events/a-russian-chinese-room-story-antedating-searle-s-1980-discussion/.

Egan, Greg (1995) *Axiomatic*. San Francisco: Nightshade Press.

Ekman, Paul (1992). "An Argument for Basic Emotions." *Cognition and Emotion* 6 (3/4): 169–200.

Feigl, Herbert (1958). "The 'mental' and the 'physical'." *Minnesota Studies in the Philosophy of Science* 2: 370–497.

Fodor, Jerry A. (1981). "The mind-body problem." *Scientific American* 244: 114–125.

French, Robert M. (1990). "Subcognition and the limits of the Turing test." *Mind* 99 (393): 53–66.

Gendler, Tamar & Hawthorne, John (2002). "Introduction." In, Tamar Gendler & John Hawthorne (eds.), *Conceivability, and Possibility*. Oxford: Oxford University Press, pp. 145–200.

Gertler, Brie (2007). "Overextending the mind." In Brie Gertler & Lawrence Shapiro (eds.), *Arguing About the Mind*. Abingdon: Routledge, pp. 192–206.

Hume, D. (1738/1978). *A Treatise of Human Nature*, 2nd edition. L.A. Selby-Bigge & P.H. Nidditch (eds.), Oxford: Clarendon Press.

Jackson, Frank (1982). "Epiphenomenal qualia." *Philosophical Quarterly* 32: 127–136.

Jackson, Frank (1986). "What Mary didn't know." *Journal of Philosophy* 83: 291–295.

Jackson, Frank (2007). "The knowledge argument, diaphonousness, representationalism." In Torin Alter & Sven Walter (eds.), *Phenomenal Concepts and Phenomenal Knowledge. New Essays on Consciousness and Physicalism*. Oxford: Oxford University Press, pp. 52–64.

James, William (1884). "What is an emotion?" *Mind* 9 (2): 188–205.

James, William (1890). *Principles of Psychology*. New York: Dover.

Kammerer, François (2015). "How a Materialist Can Deny That the United States is Probably Conscious – Response to Schwitzgebel." *Philosophia* 43 (4): 1047–1057.

Kind, Amy (2005). "Introspection." *Internet Encyclopedia of Philosophy*. Available at: https://www.iep.utm.edu/introspe/.

Kind, Amy (2015). *Persons and Personal Identity*. Cambridge: Polity Press.

Koch, Christof (2016). "How the computer beat the Go master." *Scientific American Mind* 27: 20–23.

Kurzweil, R. (2006) *The Singularity Is Near: When Humans Transcend Biology*. New York, NY: Penguin USA.

Kriegel, Uriah (2009). *Subjective consciousness*. Oxford: Oxford University Press.

Lange, Carl Georg (1885/1922). *Om sindsbevægelser: et psyko-fysiologisk Studie*. Translated by A. Haupt, as *The Emotions*. Baltimore: Williams & Wilkins.

Leckie, Ann (2013). *Ancillary Justice*. New York: Orbit Books.

Lewis, David K. (1988). "What experience teaches." *Proceedings of the Russellian Society* 13: 29–57.

Liu, Cixin (2014). *The Three Body Problem*. Translated into English by Ken Liu (2006) English Translation. New York: Tor Books.

Locke, John (1689/1975). *Essay Concerning Human Understanding*. Oxford: Oxford University Press.

Ludlow, Peter, Nagasawa, Yujin & Stoljar, Daniel (eds.) (2005). *There is something about Mary: essays on phenomenal consciousness and Frank Jackson's knowledge argument*. Cambridge, MA: MIT Press.

Macpherson, Fiona (2007). "Synaesthesia." In Mario de Caro, Francesco Ferretti & Massimo Marraffa (eds.), *Cartography of the Mind: Philosophy and Psychology in Intersection*. Dordrecht: Springer.

McEwan, Ian (2001). *Atonement*. New York: Random House.

Menary, Richard (ed.) (2010). *The Extended Mind*. Cambridge, MA: MIT Press.

Montero, Barbara (2001). "Post-physicalism." *Journal of Consciousness Studies* 8 (2): 61–80.

Nagel, Thomas (1971). "Brain bisection and the unity of consciousness." *Synthese* 22: 396–413.

Nagel, Thomas (1974). "What is it like to be a bat?" *Philosophical Review* 83: 435–450.

Nemirow, Laurence (1990). "Physicalism and the cognitive role of acquaintance." In William G. Lycan (ed.), *Mind and Cognition*. Malden Massachusetts: Blackwell.

Nozick, Robert (1974). *Anarchy, State, and Utopia*. New York: Basic Books.

Nussbaum, Martha C. (2001). *Upheavals of Thought: The Intelligence of Emotions*. Cambridge: Cambridge University Press.

Papineau, David (2002). *Thinking About Consciousness*. Oxford: Oxford University Press.

Parfit, Derek (1984). *Reasons and Persons*. Oxford: Oxford University Press.

Picard, Rosalind (1997). *Affective Computing*. Cambridge, MA: The MIT Press.

Pigliucci, Massimo (2014). "Mind uploading: a philosophical counter-analysis." In Russell Blackford & Damien Broderick (eds.), *Intelligence Unbound: The Future of Uploaded and Machine Minds*. Malden, MA: John Wiley and Sons, pp. 119–130.

Place, Ullin T. (1956). "Is consciousness a brain process." *British Journal of Psychology* 47 (1): 44–50.

Plutchik, Robert (2001). "The Nature of Emotions: Human emotions have deep evolutionary roots, a fact that may explain their complexity and provide tools for clinical practice." *American Scientist* 89(4): 344–350.

Putnam, Hilary (1960). "Minds and machines." In Sidney Hook (ed.), *Dimensions of Minds*. New York, USA: New York University Press, pp. 138–164.

Putnam, Hilary (1967). "Psychological predicates." In W. H. Capitan & D. D. Merrill (eds.), *Art, Mind, and Religion*. Pittsburgh: University of Pittsburgh Press, pp. 37–48.

Putnam, Hillary (1975). "The meaning of 'meaning'." *Minnesota Studies in the Philosophy of Science* 7: 131–193.

Rowling, J. K. (2014). *Harry Potter and the Order of the Phoenix*. London: Bloomsbury.

Russell, Bertrand (1921). *The Analysis of Mind*. New York: The Macmillan Company.

Russell, Bertrand (1927/1954). *The Analysis of Matter*. New York: Dover Publications.

Sacks, Oliver (1995). "'To see and not to see'." In Oliver Sacks, *An Anthropologist on Mars*. New York: Random House.

Schneider, Susan & Mandik, Pete (2018). "How Philosophy of Mind Can Shape the Future." In Amy Kind (ed.), *Philosophy of Mind in the Twentieth and Twenty-first Centuries*. Abingdon, Oxon: Routledge Press, pp. 303–319.

Schneider, Susan (2019). *Artificial You: AI and the Future of Your Mind*. Princeton: Princeton University Press.

Schwitzgebel, Eric (2008). "The unreliability of naive introspection." *Philosophical Review* 117 (2): 245–273.

Schwitzgebel, Eric (2015). "If materialism is true, the United States is probably conscious." *Philosophical Studies* 172 (7): 1697–1721.

Searle, John R. (1980). "Minds, brains, and programs." *Behavioral and Brain Sciences* 3 (3): 417–457.

Shapiro, Lisa (ed.) (2007). *The Correspondence Between Princess Elisabeth of Bohemia and René Descartes*. Chicago: University of Chicago Press.

Smart, J. J. C. (1959). "Sensations and brain processes." *Philosophical Review* 68 (April): 141–156.

Sober, Elliott (2015). *Ockham's Razors: A User's Manual*. Cambridge: Cambridge University Press.

Solomon, Robert C. (1976). *The Passions*. Garden City, New York: Doubleday Anchor.

Sorensen, Roy A. (1992). *Thought Experiments*. New York: Oxford University Press USA.

Sperry, Roger (1968). "Hemisphere deconnection and unity in conscious awareness." *American Psychologist* 23: 722–733.

tich, S. P. (1978). "Do Animals Have Beliefs?" *Australasian Journal of Philosophy* 57: 15–28.

toljar, Daniel (2017). "Physicalism." *The Stanford Encyclopedia of Philosophy* (Winter Edition), Edward N. Zalta (ed.). Available at: https://plato.stanford.edu/archives/win2017/entries/physicalism/.

toljar, Daniel (2006). *Ignorance and Imagination: The Epistemic Origin of the Problem of Consciousness*. New York: Oxford University Press USA.

utton, Lee (1959). "Soul mate." Reprinted in Michael Philips (1984), *Philosophy and Science Fiction*. Amherst, NY: Prometheus Books.

ononi, Giulio (2012). "Integrated information theory of consciousness: an updated account." *Archives Italiennes de Biologie* 150 (2–3): 56–90.

uring, Alan M. (1950). "Computing machinery and intelligence." *Mind* 59 (October): 433–460.

Jarwick, Kevin (2002). "Cyborg 1.0." Available at: https://www.wired.com/2000/02/warwick/.

Jeiskopf, Daniel A. (2008). "Patrolling the mind's boundaries." *Erkenntnis* 68 (2): 265–276.

Wilkes, Kathleen V. (1988). *Real People: Personal Identity Without Thought Experiments*. Oxford: Oxford University Press.

elazy, Roger (2002). "For a Breath I Tarry." In Roger Zelazny, *The Last Defender of Camelot*. New York: Simon and Schuster, pp. 18–64.

INDEX

9 781138 807822